Dog-wise

What We Learn From Dogs

Judith Wright

ISBN:-10:1544639007
ISBN-13:978-15445 39000

For Liam, who changed me

CONTENTS

ACKNOWLEDGMENTS

My sincere thanks to the contributors of these chapters—you know who you are. The book could not have been written without you. A special thanks to Arlette Seib, who shared from her original work on guardian and herding dogs, provided many key insights, and gave generously of her time, editing skills and expertise. Thanks, too, to Jill Werle, who introduced me to many of the dog people in these chapters; your encouragement was appreciated at the early stages of the project. Kristina Rothstein, thank you for editing the manuscript and for your long-term enthusiasm. Jill Robinson, thanks for reviewing early drafts and excerpts, and for your encouragement. Will Rogers, thank you for your proof-reading skills *extraordinaire*. And to Berta Bindle, Shelly and Doug Borrowman, thanks for last minute favors.

A special thanks to the photographers: Johane Janelle (www.johanejanelle.com) for the cover image and to James R Page (www.flickr.com/photos/pageworld/) for the author photo. For your cover design, Tracy Creighton, I thank you.

Two excerpts from *Dog-wise* were first published in Prairies North Magazine (2016) and the Western Producer (2017).

PROLOGUE

A few years ago, my son and I adopted a coyote hound, a mixed-breed greyhound from a pack of greyhound-wolfhound crosses seized by the Saskatchewan SPCA. What started as a mission to understand and rehabilitate this dog turned into an exploration of the wider dog world and the special bond people share with dogs.

This book is a collection of reflections by dog people about what dogs teach us. Anyone who is a dog person recognizes other dog people—people with the special ability to read between the lines of dog behaviour. They are people who have found a unique connection with dogs and appreciate the dog mind. Whether they know it or not, they view the world just a little bit differently than others.

I owe the name of this book to an acquaintance of mine who described the subtle differences between types of dog people. "Myself, I'm a Lab man," he said. "Even when I haven't had a Golden or a black Lab for a few years, dog-wise, I'm strictly about the retrievers." He went on to make some interesting claims about dogs and their owners: bulldogs are determined and persistent, their owners like board games; German shepherds are

1

protective, shepherd owners will do anything for their friends; huskies are strong willed, husky owners love sports; dachshunds are stubborn and brave, their people are bossy. And so on.

I was aware of the distinction between cat people and dog people, but this was the first time I'd considered differences in canine owners—as if each were a breed apart. There is some truth to the joke that our dogs resemble us, that we tend to choose pets with features as familiar as the face we see daily in the mirror. Aside from projecting one's own personality on one's pet (also known as the tail wagging the dog), we do seem to seek companions of compatible character and temperament. There is an inclination for people who have enjoyed the company of a particular dog to choose that breed over and over again—to try to replace, even, that first beloved dog in colour, shape and size, in search of that one special companion.

Some people become devotees of a single breed, others practice informed discrimination. Then there are the generalists, mixed-mutt lovers, perhaps best described as individualists who seek certain canine personalities beyond the breed markers. It made a kind of crude sense to me, when I first contemplated this project, that dog people who discover a particular connection to one kind of dog may intuit some special kind of wisdom from the experience.

If dogs make us human, as some people suggest, then what a particular dog has to teach us is worth understanding.

The task I set for myself was to talk to a score of dog owners and professional handlers about their dogs, to observe them with their dogs, and ask what is special about each. This book is about what people have learned from loving, working and living with a dog.

1 HOW IT BEGAN

-The importance of letting go-

I was brought into the dog world reluctantly. A few years ago, I would have described myself as an affirmed cat person. My son was the one who wanted a dog. I didn't want a dog for the usual reasons: they tie you down, they make a mess, they bark. I didn't *dislike* dogs— I'd grown up with family dogs and I liked other people's dogs—but deep down I thought of dogs as major luggage.

Dogs require serious commitment, as I explained to Liam—fifteen, that summer, and desperate for a dog. He had always wanted a dog, had pined for a dog. To give him credit, he'd done his research and narrowed his choice to the greyhound, which he presented to me as more of a big cat than a dog. The greyhound is called the forty-mile-an-hour couch potato, good for short bursts of speed and then typically inert. Part of the sighthound family, including wolfhounds, deerhounds, Afghans, Salukis and whippets, they're quiet dogs and enjoy fairly robust health. They don't suffer from hip dysplasia or other congenital problems common in large dogs. The disadvantages of the breed seemed fairly minimal to me—a coat that continually sheds, and a tendency for poor recall.

To sweeten the deal, Liam promised to commit some of his new weekend salary to help cover the cost of keeping a large dog. He found a couple of greyhound-crosses at the local SPCA. I wondered whether we shouldn't consider getting a purebred. We found the website of the nearest greyhound rescue group, an Alberta group specializing in re-homing ex-racers. That summer, several race tracks in the western U.S. had closed, and with fewer kennels, no ex-racers were available. There were, however, a few coyote hounds up for adoption—what they called mixed-breed greyhounds or lurchers. These dogs were part of a large seizure from Saskatchewan. That sounded familiar.

In Saskatoon, where we were living at the time, the SPCA had been overwhelmed by the size of the seizure, so some of the dogs were sent to shelters in Edmonton and Calgary. Several of these dogs then "failed" in the Alberta shelters, and the rescue organization agreed to foster them out among their members. "Failed" should have been the tip-off.

What I remember most about our adoption interview was the emphasis placed on keeping the dog on a leash at all times. Greyhounds don't have good recall—this was repeated several times—they have a strong drive to run, are nine-tenths instinct, and are not trained to return.

It was hard to judge the dogs from their online pictures. Our contact pointed to one dog she had in mind for us. He was sturdier than a greyhound, fawn-colored, with dark shepherd-ish markings on the face. The dog's bio read: *Initially somewhat insecure. Doesn't appear to have been walked on leash but he picks up the rudiments quickly. Cat-safe. A diamond in the ruff.*

Like many a prospective adopter, I believed my experience with family dogs would serve us well enough. I'd done my share of dog-walking and puppy obedience, enough to know how much time and effort would be required. Truthfully, any rationale was moot because, as Liam put it, "Aw, come-on-mom. He needs us."

We drove to Olds, Alberta, to meet the dog.

***

He was a big tall fellow, deep-chested and built like an athlete, all muscle and sinew. When we entered the backyard through the gate, he shrank against the fence, licking his lips and blowing softly through his teeth. At this point, the dog was still nameless. His foster-dad, Bill, eventually enticed him into the house, where Liam tried unsuccessfully to feed him. "He's not much motivated by treats," Bill said.

Bill's wife, Shauna, invited me into the living room to give them some space to get acquainted. A scrapbook on the coffee table displayed Bill and Shauna's foster dogs, a dozen or more elegant-looking ex-track dogs that had been successfully adopted over the years. "They're all so different," Shauna said encouragingly. "Some of them have never been inside a house, and they can't walk on smooth floors or climb stairs. Some can't relieve themselves on leash. It takes time."

Bill and Shauna's own well-mannered greyhound, Pebbles, sniffed at my shoes. Shauna told me Pebbles helped to smooth the way for their fosters. "Greyhounds are pack animals," she said, "and they're pretty relaxed about taking in others. One thing is for sure, the dog you're getting has perfect pack manners. And he's got great teeth. I don't know what they were feeding him."

It was late in the day so we retreated to the hotel to sleep on our decision. The irony of driving to another province to see a dog that Liam had probably pointed out, weeks earlier at the local shelter, did not escape me. The conclusion could only be that we were meant to have this dog.

It did cross my mind that we might be getting more dog than we could handle. In the hotel room the next morning, Liam announced the dog's new name. "His name is Tove," he said firmly. An hour later Bill was trying to trick Tove into the back seat of our car. Bill climbed through one door and exited through the other, trapping the dog neatly on the seats in between. "How do we get him back inside if he has to get out to pee?" I asked. It was an eight hour drive back to Saskatoon.

"Oh he loves car rides," Bill said. "He'll probably hop right back in."

Probably. Right. The dog took up the entire back seat. When Liam reached back to reassure him with a pat, the dog's eyes rolled in terror.

The dog approached his food with suspicion. He had to be invited to eat. When he did, he nibbled furtively, reluctantly—almost as if being inconvenienced. Our cat watched balefully, having made her dominion clear from the start.

We put the dog dish on top of the dog-food barrel so that Tove wouldn't have to reach down to eat. One day, he deliberately knocked the bowl off the barrel, and the stainless-steel bowl clattered on the floor. The following day, he did it again; he deliberately picked up the bowl and dropped it on the floor. From then on, he behaved as if he was terrified of the bowl. We had to spread his kibble on the floor to get him to eat.

We had been warned that he might hide in a bedroom for a few days. Greyhounds are sensitive, we had learned. Tove didn't leave Liam's room for a week, except for his twice-daily walks. Outside on the sidewalk, he frequently froze, and if we encouraged him in an unfamiliar direction he dissolved into a seventy-pound puddle of distress. Then there was no budging him until he was ready to quick-march back to the house.

His list of phobias grew daily: bicycles, children, joggers, trucks, trains, overpasses, underpasses, sprinklers, radios, television, fans, the house furnace. At first, all this seemed to be understandable in a rescued dog, but, in addition to being fearful, the dog seemed sad. He kept to himself. In unguarded moments he stretched out on the floor like a lion on his haunches, his torso twisted, his head on the floor. He looked like he'd been hit by a truck. At night, we heard him creeping around the house, exploring under cover of darkness.

I called the rescue organization, I called his foster home. What could they tell me about this dog's past? Give him time, they reassured me—but after ten days of this behaviour I started to feel the milk of human kindness curdle a little. Come on, dog, you've been rescued, I wanted to tell him, as I sat on the floor beside him, drinking innumerable cups of tea. He ignored me as completely as he ignored Liam.

Another worrying fact: the dog refused to drink from a bowl of any kind. He was happy to drink from the pond in the garden at night, but refused to drink during the day. When a sudden snowstorm froze the pond in our backyard, he began to gulp down snow.

Then, about two weeks after he arrived, he started to itch. He scratched and scratched and nibbled himself from tail to toe. On the same day, Liam broke into a rash and started to sneeze. I dosed them both with Benadryl and made their respective medical appointments.

Liam's rash went away as soon as we banished the dog from his bedroom. For twenty-four itch-free hours, the medication seemed to work for the dog too—and then the itching returned as strongly as ever. Our vet assured me he was lice-free and flea-free. She de-wormed him for good measure, and suggested he might have food allergies. I had better find out what he'd been fed in the past so I could avoid the ingredients. Find out as much as you can about the dog's background, she advised, and that will help you to get a handle on the other issues.

But when I contacted the SPCA I was told the file couldn't be shared because criminal charges were pending. We didn't know whether Tove had been abused or neglected. We were committed, but confused.

Since dogs are "forever," we, as his "forever home," had to figure him out. For twelve weeks, his behaviour baffled me; he was fearful but docile, shy but stubborn, nervous but lazy, and as different from any dog I'd ever met as another species. He remained tenaciously aloof, and the only time he sought our company was, bizarrely, when one of us played the piano. Then he stretched out on the floor like a sounding board, but gave no other sign of pleasure.

One thing he did enjoy was to be brushed; he would lean into me then, as if he had a knot that needed loosening. He gave the cat a wide berth and was not territorial. He politely abstained from *fetch,* and didn't play with toys.

And so I went about trying to fix him as if he was a problem.

His undefined past became my obsession. When I tried to picture his life, chained to a few square feet of ground (this much his foster-home had learned), there were plenty of things that didn't add up. On the one hand, he was so skittish that he might never have been inside a house. On the other hand, he was completely comfortable with stairs and smooth floors. He was particularly devoted to soft piles of laundry and to beds—he had started to creep into mine in the middle of the night, which I took as a positive sign. He was deaf to the command, *come,* but had a sound understanding of *off* and *up*. He loved riding in cars; sometimes I had to leave him in the back seat with the windows down because he wouldn't get out.

Liam spent the first few weeks Googling potential solutions to behavioural oddities, and then became mildly indifferent to the dilemma. My own personal response to challenge has always been to read. The deeper I got into the dog literature, the more questions I had.

It was not that the dog was out of control, he simply wasn't *there*. Obedience classes were out of the question. He was far too reclusive to tolerate strangers. He was good on the leash and didn't pull, but Liam was starting to have difficulties at walk times because Tove sat down regularly on the sidewalk and wouldn't budge. Plus there were other signs of growing assertiveness.

The day we took Tove to the off-leash dog park he began his transformation. He was a different dog when he was off the leash. He *danced*, he *pranced*, on spring-board feet. And he *ran*—it was breathtaking to watch him. His speed and grace were unmatched.

He was confident with other dogs, could approach the butchest-looking dog in the dog park and diffuse any signs of aggression in seconds—not by a show of submissiveness, but by nosing around, turning away, looking at something else, or just standing tall and still, with the tip of his tail wagging (*not* the *hale fellow well met* signal I thought it meant).

Sometimes these encounters ended with Tove slowly and stiffly walking away from the other dog, and sometimes they turned into the little play-bow invitation. When play did follow—and only with dogs of comparable build and weight—the game turned into a pell-mell chase, in which Tove dominated with power and speed.

Usually, he brought the other dog tumbling down at top velocity. If a third and fourth dog got into the action the whole game deteriorated into a melee, with relentless badgering of the dog down, loud yelping, and alarmed owners wading in to rescue their dogs. To make matters worse, throughout the game Tove kept up a growly bark— we'd never heard him bark until then. The more dogs involved in the scrum, the more self-assured he behaved.

Later, I learned that sighthounds were bred to hunt in packs and, unlike gun dogs, do not need human accomplices; they hunt and kill quite efficiently on their own.

Needless to say, I started to pick my times at the dog parks more carefully, when the dog traffic was light.

I knew I needed more hands-on advice to rehabilitate

him. In truth, I wasn't sure if it was Tove that needed help or *me* who needed re-educating. Aside from the dog park experience, part of me was already adjusting to him, learning to accept, even to admire his oddness. I shared an ice-cream cone with him in the car one afternoon, a few months after he'd arrived. He didn't relish the treat, but seemed to accept it to please me. The delicacy with which he licked the cone almost brought tears to my eyes.

Perhaps the dog had something to teach me.

Coming to this humbling conclusion—that I really knew *nothing* about dogs—was what prompted me to start at the beginning. What exactly might one expect from different dog breeds? How much behaviour was "hard-wired" and how much malleable?

I remember the evening I decided to take this new approach because it was the same evening I let Tove run free—really free—for the first time. The off-leash area at Chief Whitecap Park runs along the river margin, a place of deep bush and shifting sandbars. The park is unfenced and the trails are far from the roads. I knew I was taking a chance letting him run free there. I knew Liam wouldn't approve. I knew it might take hours to get Tove back—I might lose him altogether.

But it was a beautiful evening, early in the spring, with the cottonwoods budding on the floodplain. A string of returning geese flew overhead. I could feel the dog wanting to run. As I stood beside him, I considered my task.

Finding myself about to chart unfamiliar territory with a companion I'd thought of as familiar struck me as perhaps one of the best life-lesson opportunities I could find. Reaching down, I unsnapped the leash from Tove's collar. For a moment, unaware he was free, he continued to walk beside me.

Then, as confident of his direction as the wind, he ran.

2 SHOW DOGS

-Ye shall know them by their dogs-

I started my mission by casting the net broadly. Where could I meet a lot of people who were knowledgeable about a lot of dog breeds at once? Not only would a dog show provide a broad cross-section of breeds and experienced handlers, there had to be plenty of nervous if not neurotic show dogs from which to draw comparisons.

I had some vague prejudices against dog shows, but a work colleague of mine was involved in the Canadian Kennel Club and she agreed to be my guide. Jill had trained and shown Shetland sheepdogs since the 1970's, and she had always struck me as a down-to-earth sort of person. Jill was fun-loving and sensible. If anyone could cure me of my uneducated bias it would be Jill.

On a November afternoon, at the Prince Albert Exhibition grounds, two hundred people and about one hundred and fifty dogs were jammed together in a small hall. The two show rings took up about a quarter of the hall, and around them eddied the untidy trappings of the dog show: stacked portable kennels, grooming tables, brushes, spray bottles, coolers, half-eaten lunches, racks of fancy show collars, training shoes, electrical cords, lawn chairs—all higgledy-piggelty in unsightly disarray.

If the world of pedigree conformation is all about

appearances, a surprising degree of tunnel vision was the norm here. All the focus was on the dog—which was as it should be. Jill's own dogs were at home (they'd already earned their championships) but her sister, Peggy, had a dog entered in the show. Ace was working on his championship, but he wouldn't be in the ring for a while.

The dogs were all coiffed and trimmed and groomed to within an inch of—well, *ridiculous* came to mind. To my uninformed eye, the dogs looked bored. A giant poodle with a topiary-like hair-style lay on top of his crate, looking as if he had died of boredom. A pair of Great Danes stood in the aisle beside me, waiting their turn in the ring. I couldn't resist admiring them, whatever my personal feelings about their cropped ears (which looked like gently tapered antennae). What was in it for them?

The answer was treats. Lots of them. I was taken aback to see a handler pulling treats from her—*mouth* ? She wasn't the only one. "It's to get the dog to look at them," Jill whispered, "to keep them focused." They aren't... uh, doggie treats, then? "No, usually just cheese, liver or wieners."

Some of the competitors sported huge wad-like bulges in their cheeks. The minute a dog and handler entered the ring, the hunt for treats began—from pockets, sleeves, bosoms, every possible nook and cranny. The dogs jerked and craned, following the trajectory of the treats, hypnotized by the handlers' constant fussing hand movements.

A *frisson* of excitement hardly described it.

Most of the handlers were women, and everyone seemed to be wearing a business suit, even the male handlers with gun dogs. Among the female handlers the tight pencil skirt was the outfit of choice and a more impractical uniform couldn't be imagined. Many handlers were up and down on their knees, extending a paw here, a tail there. Don't get me wrong—I very much *liked* that these people were so focused on the perfection of their dogs—but so far the dog show smacked of neither class, glamour or even distinction. In fact, it all seemed quite ordinary.

Still keen to shed my misgivings and to embrace the dog show, I tried to concentrate on the program. The crowd jostled around me. A new batch of competitors entered the show ring. After the *go-around,* everyone stopped to grope for a treat. Jill kept up a running commentary.

First, the *quick look* by the judges, then the *examination,* up on the table. Now, looking into the mouth (and for some breeds counting the teeth), feeling the coat, the angulation of their shoulders, their bone structure, the length of the tail. Then, on the floor for the *down and back* and another go-around. "What the judge doesn't want to see is *bump, bump, bump,* but rather a smooth movement with a little convergence," Jill whispered, "and just a little bit of angulation from the shoulder, the hip coming in towards the center. "

The class changed and a great deal of commotion followed. Jill and Peggy held a hushed conference about the "bred by exhibitor" class. Jill explained the combinations and permutations of the scoring system, but she was starting to lose me. Points were awarded toward *Winner, Best of Winner, Best of Group,* and *Best Bitch.* Everyone was working towards a *Championship,* a *Permit,* a *Major* or a *Judging Paper.* It sounded to me like a cross between Dragons Den and a pyramid scheme.

We passed a handler who was applying hairspray to a dog on a grooming table. The dog's head was encased in a sequenced bag to spare its sensitive nose from the clouds of sticky mist. Jill, just out of hearing range, remarked, "Some people put chalk in the dog's coat to make the hair look whiter, or to make it stand off the body more. There's lots of product used. The Canadian Kennel Club says, *Thou shalt not use hairspray*—actually they say *there shall be no foreign product in the coat.* It's a rule that is generally ignored. Given current expectations, no one can show a poodle without a lot of hairspray."

Appearances aside, one thing seemed clear to me: the dog show wasn't a spectator sport. There was a dismaying lack of seating in the hall—just one ragged row of folding chairs set up around the ring, like an afterthought. My feet were killing me; now I knew why the handlers wore running shoes with their business suits. A few foot-sore husbands watched from the sidelines. A string of quarreling children wilted in the aisle, waiting for the Junior Handler event.

So much for learning anything about the different breeds. My first attempt to question a handler—the one with her dog's head in the grooming noose—faltered. After a few more tries at pleasantries with busy handlers, I began to suspect I'd never penetrate the cult. I sank into a folding chair and studied Jill's show catalogue, which might have been written in Esperanto.

It crossed my mind, after the dog show, that if food was the ultimate reward—and one could coax any behaviour with food—Tove was going to be a hard case to train. Being unmotivated by treats had, however, earned him more of my respect. I wasn't feeling very positive about the dog-show experience, but what did a championship show-dog look like when he was at home?

I was at Jill's door the following Saturday for a debrief. I had left Tove at home. Nine-year-old Pilgrim gave me the loud official Sheltie welcome. Nomad, Jill's fourteen-year-old blue merle Sheltie, looked on with dignity from the living room. After we settled on the sofa, Pilgrim seized a rawhide bone from under the coffee table. He meant to finish it before Catcher, who had been left in the yard, discovered his prize. Catcher was the latest addition to Jill's Sheltie family ("There are testosterone issues between those two," she said darkly).

In preparation for the dog show I had read up on the Canadian Kennel Club, the association that regulates most official pedigree dog shows in Canada. The CKC, as it is known, is a member-run non-profit registry for purebred dogs, and Jill and her husband, John, were club "lifers." The CKC tracks pedigrees, promotes shows for purebreds, and awards championships and other titles in CKC competitions. The Club currently recognizes 175 dog breeds. For a dog to be registered, the dog's dam and sire must be registered. The Club recognizes mixed breeds for certain trials, as does its American counterpart, the AKC. CKC members are permitted to breed only CKC recognized breeds, and they sign a membership pledge not to engage in the buying, selling or breeding of dogs not purebred. If it sounds like an exclusive club it is, but there are over 17,000 members across the country.

All three of Jill's Shelties were CKC Conformation Champions. The Conformation class was originally designed to show off a breeder's stock, so the judging is all about how closely the dog conforms to the breed standard. This includes how closely the dog conforms to the popular colour and "type" of the day. When I asked Jill what was needed to compete in this class, she said, "You need a dog that is close to the standard for starters. Shelties have to be no shorter than thirteen inches at the shoulder, and no taller than sixteen inches. Once they get over sixteen inches, they're done."

The smallest detail of the dog's appearance is crucial in the Conformation class. For example, Shelties' ears are important, because they change the way the dog looks. Dogs with tipped ears are a little sweeter-looking in expression. She pulled out a hefty photo album, full of pictures of family Shelties, dating back to the 1950's. Hoisting it open on the coffee table, she pointed: here was Teddy, with vertical ears. Not show material.

"Basically," Jill said, "to compete in this event, you have to start with a dog with the potential for being the right size, and being nicely put together, so they'll move very well. That means finding a knowledgeable breeder, because those characteristics aren't visible to most of us when the dog is a pup."

Pilgrim, I learned, came from a trusted breeder in Nova Scotia. Jill had only seen pictures of the dam and sire. She went on to say that not all Shelties were beautiful-moving dogs. When I asked her what a beautiful-moving Sheltie looked like, she had a very precise picture in mind.

"For herding dogs, with the exception of border collies, when you watch the dog trot, their top line should be pretty smooth, and their legs should have a nice balanced reach. If they're too short in the forearm they won't have much reach, and may flip their front legs up. You want nice smooth movement."

I felt a bit disappointed; this was still sounding very superficial. There had to be more to show dogs than this. I pressed on with my questions, determined to get to the heart of the show dog.

How did Jill get into showing dogs in the first place? She'd been hooked on performance back in the 80's when she had an incredibly smart and easy-to-train Sheltie named Missy. At that time, the CKC only offered conformation and obedience competitions for Shelties. One year, Missy got an obedience trial championship and was Number Ten Working and Herding dog in Canada without Jill even trying. They were just going to shows for fun.

Today, as she pointed out, there are many different categories of CKC competition. Rally obedience and agility competitions are great crowd-pleasers; draft competitions (dog pulling carts) are popular; in tracking competitions the dog finds elements laid on a track; then, there are herding trials—sheep, cattle and ducks.

Did you say ducks?

She explained.

There are certain breeds of ducks that are more likely

to group together than others, which makes them ideal for herding. "If you're stock handling for a duck trial, you pick your little group of ducks, and you fluff them up a bit to see if they'll group or take off in different directions. If they stick together, they make the cut." Jill said this to me with an entirely straight face.

She named a few other classes of CKC competition for specific breeds, such as lure-coursing for sighthounds, earth dog trials for terriers, and hunting trials for sporting dogs. Jill's husband, John, had a pair of Alaskan Malamutes. John was a former CKC Director, so he and Jill had either attended or competed in most of these competitions.

It was hard for me to imagine the sweet and diminutive Pilgrim, Conformation Champion (who admittedly was doing great violence to the rawhide bone under the table), getting up to anything as grimy and potentially risky as herding sheep, but he did have several herding titles. Now, *herding*—that interested me.

Jill described some of the skills that CKC sheep trial competitors work on in herding clinics. The sheepdog's desire to please (its bid ability) is what makes herding dogs popular as pets. She agreed that border collies are super-intelligent, and biddable second to none, but who really wants to live full-time with a high energy border collie?

Shelties, she claimed, are usually more mellow. As for the kind of people attracted to Shelties? "People generally like the size and the look of them. Some Shelties bark a lot. Pilgrim barks when he's having a great time, or when there's a lot of pressure to get sheep out of a corner."

Dog trials and dog shows, she pointed out, aren't just about competition. They are very much social occasions. "Really there are three kinds of people who are attracted to the dog show world. People who love their dog and want other people to see how good they are, people doing it for companionship—because people develop friends in the dog world. The third type are there for ego. We want our dogs to look good, perform well, and beat other dogs!"

Was it fair to say that dog shows attracted some—well, eccentric types? Jill laughed and said she thought most dog show people were pretty reasonable; they might think other dogs weren't as good as their's, or the judge was blind, but they'd accept losing a competition. "You know, you pay your money for an opinion, but you don't have to agree with it. But there *are* a few folks who really *are* over the top. Like the ones who disturb your dog's stack."

Okay, your *stack*?

"They run up or step into your dog from behind and disturb your dog's stack! Make him anxious." Jill demonstrated by retrieving Pilgrim from under the table. She placed his feet squarely on the floor in a slightly extended stance to display his shape. "You stand the dog like this. Stand, now! See, that's it. And you try to get him to show off." She made an elaborate hand gesture to attract his gaze. "And of course he'd be groomed to the nines, and he'd show his ears and wag his tail at the judge."

But Pilgrim wasn't having any of it. He scurried back to the rawhide bone. Unfazed, Jill fell back on the sofa, laughing.

What had the dogs taught her? "That's a good question," she said, and considered her answer. "That I have more ego than I probably should have. I was more competitive in the past. Now, as soon as the dog get its conformation championship, I don't bother anymore with that competition. Conformation is not a priority for me. Missy was so easy to train and she did so well, but every once in a while she'd fail—and it doesn't take much to fail. A *sit-stay* needs to be for three minutes. One time, she lay down; I can still remember it. I was so mad at her when we left the ring, I had to give her leash to my dad. But that episode *did* influence my thinking, later on."

She paused. "You know, they're only dogs. They don't know why they have to sit there for three darned minutes. They're bored and they're tired. There's really nothing in it for them. It took me a while, but I learned that I have ego, and at times a bad temper. I'm very conscious that the dogs are only doing this because I'm asking them to."

I thought about the Great Danes at the dog show and echoed her skepticism. Most likely they were kindly handled, and it was clear to me that many handlers, like Jill, gave their dogs ample room to express their personalities. Nomad was in the habit of barking at her—even nipping, she confessed—if he thought she'd done something wrong on the agility course. "If I direct him with my body differently from what I tell him, he'll just say, 'Right. I'm doing my own course now.'"

At one point Missy had given up on a utility exercise, after she had been unable to distinguish between a pile of twelve dumbbells and the one with Jill's fresh scent on it. Missy brought the wrong dumbbell to Jill. "'No,' I told her—I wasn't even mad—I just said, 'No.' She just dropped it. It took me three months to get her back out there on that exercise again. I think she just thought, 'Well, I'm right and she's wrong.' And who knows, maybe the dumbbell she picked up was every bit as strongly scented as the one I set out for her to find. I mean, they were *all* my dumbbells. I think she was just confused, so she didn't want to do it anymore."

About ninety percent of Jill's friends are dog people. "I think people who have dogs understand the value of dogs as family members, and have common values. It's a way for people to spend time with their dogs, and to work on something that is mutually enjoyable. It's active, it's fun, and showing is something the whole family can get involved in. It's like one big family."

Okay, one slightly eccentric family.

3 FAMILY DOGS

-Awareness, self-control...and taking it as it comes-

The dog show was clearly a case of casting the net too widely. I needed to look for advice closer to home. Within my own circle of friends, the two dogs most familiar to me were Eddie and Luca, the family dogs of my friends, Judy and Jeff.

Judy and Jeff are an easy-going couple who live on an acreage outside Saskatoon. Jeff loves blues music and is a builder, and Judy enjoys gardening and volunteering with the local environmental society. Their dogs, friendly and well-socialized, were raised from puppyhood in a busy household with four children. Eddie is a female St Bernard, and Luca, a female bearded collie. They aren't working dogs—Luca doesn't herd anything but the grandchildren, and Eddie has never rescued anyone. They aren't super-obedient dogs, but as companion animals their manners are those of the "good citizen."

On a warm spring afternoon we chatted about the dogs on the porch. Eddie, short for Edina Monsoon (from the hit British television series, *Absolutely Fabulous*) lay in a heap at Jeff's feet, like a hundred pounds of hot bricks, and Luca lay curled at Judy's feet, chasing her own dream butterflies. The poplar stands and scrub bush beyond the house were full of rabbits—which is why this was one of Tove's favorite destinations. He was out there now, in the bush, being his usual antisocial self, exercising the rabbits. There *were* coyotes in the hills but it was the rabbits that kept him occupied.

How *do* we end up with the dogs we do? My question was a good starting point. Like asking couples how they met, this led to some interesting revelations. Jeff admitted that he'd never even *seen* a St Bernard up close before he met Eddie. "We saw an ad in the paper," he said. "*St Bernard puppies. Ready to go. Serious inquiries only.*" "Were we serious?" Judy asked Jeff.

They both wanted an outdoor dog for the acreage, partly for predator control. "At first I thought we needed one of those great big dogs that kills wolves to protect your sheep," Jeff said. The breeder who placed the ad for the St Bernard puppies turned out to be an old family friend, so they told themselves they were driving out for a visit.

"But you don't see St Bernard puppies and then think, 'Na, we were thinking of something else,'" Jeff said.

Luca, the bearded collie, is the perfect example of how your practical research evaporates when you spot the dog of your dreams. Judy had in mind a short-haired easy-care dog they would get around the holidays when there was extra time to spend with a new dog. Then she made the mistake of picking up a dog magazine that featured the adorable-looking bearded collie. The nearest breeder was in Calgary and when she called she learned one pup from the litter was left—saved for someone who now couldn't take it. Judy's son just happened to be driving to Calgary that weekend.

"It was February, this wasn't the holidays, and this wasn't a short-haired dog," Judy laughed.

Having dogs has always been part of their family life. "There's something about dogs and families that is pretty basic," Judy said. Their four children are now grown and have families of their own, but the house is full of kids and grandkids, siblings and friends, on the weekends. Jeff suggested that important values, like responsibility, are reinforced by having a dog in the family. Judy, however, thought otherwise. She ruefully recalled what had happened when she thought their son needed a dog.

"With two adults and four kids, the dog just tends to gravitate to the mom. The dog didn't really reinforce anything. None of us had time for the dog, other than feeding her and an occasional walk."

But of course, time must be found, and the task often falls to the main care-giver. Plus the dog typically aligns itself with the head of the household—this much I'd learned from Tove. In-as-far as he had shown an interest in either of us, he was sticking closer to me these days than to Liam. Luckily, Liam had taken this in stride. He was a busy teenager.

I had also discovered by now that a new dog will jockey for second position after the household head— which includes competing with the children. This explained Tove's ongoing truculence with Liam at walk time.

Judy agreed with me, that *in spite* of our efforts to delegate authority to children, the dog chooses its leader and not the other way around.

The dog *chooses* you; there is more than a little truth to this statement. Luca, the herder, was Judy's dog; Judy was the shepherd of children and household tasks. Eddie was Jeff's dog and lived mostly outside; Eddie, like Jeff, presided over the garage, the workshop and the yard.

It was hard for me to imagine Eddie ever having been small. She wasn't large for a St Bernard but she had a commanding presence. She showed a bit of protective behaviour—she barked at the coyotes—but she wasn't, strictly speaking, a watch dog. Her size was a deterrent to intruders but not her personality. She was the classic easy-going Saint. She didn't come down the driveway to greet everyone personally, as Luca did, and she didn't seem to crave attention. It had never been clear to me whether Eddie or Luca was the alpha dog. Like Judy and Jeff in their household, each seemed to lead at a different time.

Luca was Eddie's senior by a few years. The two dogs didn't share the same space most of the time; Luca preferred the indoors, and Eddie outdoors, so they rarely needed to sort out their rank. I had seen, on occasion, each dog defer politely to the other, and it made me wonder: how does one raise polite and respectful dogs?

Some of the time-honored theories of dog dominance and submission, modeled on what we thought we knew about wolves, has been revisited in recent years. I spent a bit of time looking into this. The dominance model that once held ground turns out to have been based on observations of wolves held in captivity. Unrelated animals that are forced to live together aren't typical in the wild, especially among wolves. Rank, within a free wild wolf unit, usually the family unit, turns out to be a much less obvious construct.

Paralleling this new understanding of pack dynamics, the new working model for dog training is "parenting". Whether or not this is because we're a parent-focused culture is hard to say. It's difficult to step outside our own human-centric perspective.

The old dominance model of training certainly mimics our old human hierarchies and power structures. Not that dominance and submission don't exist for dogs—they are very important to pack relations. Some experts don't recommend keeping more than two unrelated dogs, unless you are prepared to act as permanent referee. Dogs, like their ancestors, are wired to protect scarce resources from competitors. Puppies that grow up together, or grow up with human pack members, have their place defined and reinforced throughout their lifetime. Perhaps simply growing up from puppyhood in a large well-mannered family was why Eddie and Luca were such agreeable and non-contentious dogs.

Jeff told me that Eddie sometimes tried to take a stand with other dogs, but she wasn't very good at it. "Visiting dogs easily get the upper hand. She's quite take-it-as-it-comes about it—social, but not like Luca. Luca likes to be where the family herd is."

Whenever Tove and I visited the acreage Tove seemed to defer to Luca and know not pester her with play invitations. His overtures to Eddie, on the other hand, were endless. Eddie and Luca were both older than Tove by almost half a dozen years. Eddie didn't like Tove's rough play, and usually stuck close to me for protection. I often ended up putting one of the three on the leash, just to keep the peace. Oddly enough, all three dogs competed to be on the leash.

It surprised me that, given their free run of eighty acres, the dogs still got excited when it was time for a walk. The desire to be with us and to respect a human leader are two characteristics that distinguish dogs from wolves. Dogs are perpetual dependents and perpetually attention-craving, like permanent puppies. Genetically speaking, dogs are programmed to remain emotional youngsters. Certainly, then, "parenting" is a more appropriate training model than dominance.

On the subject of upbringing and good manners Jeff said, "If you aren't going to train a dog to show respect and to behave and to listen to you, then you don't want to own a St Bernard. A dog that size can do a lot of damage. They're one of the top breeds involved in human injuries. Most of that is probably just from getting knocked over."

Eddie had been quite easy to train but that wasn't always a given with Saints. As with any purebred line, undesirable behavioural traits sometimes coincide with desired physical traits. "There are dogs that no matter what you do, you can't get past their genetic traits," Jeff said. In his view, good behaviour in dogs wasn't just a matter of obedience.

Elizabeth Marshall Thomas, an anthropologist, and perhaps my favorite dog-book writer, suggested that dogs learn as much from our example as from our conscious effort to train them. She preferred to keep dog training to a minimum. "When I don't train them, they train me," she wrote in *The Hidden Life of Dogs*.

Only when we don't train dogs to be obedience robots can we see what they're really like—this was her suggestion. Other knowledgeable dog people also note that the dogs with the best manners—the ones whose owners aren't constantly giving them orders—are the dogs that are most comfortable within their human pack.

Well-mannered dogs rarely need to be reprimanded. They aren't unruly, they don't challenge and continually disobey. They have found their place in their social environment and they feel secure.

When I asked Jeff what living with dogs had taught him he said, "With dogs, you become more aware of what's going on around you. First you become more aware of those behavioural messages. As with children, behaviour is part of communication. If Luca is wiggling around, I wonder what's going on and look around and see, 'Oh, her water dish is empty.' Also, I find that when you tune in to one thing, you tune in to many things." He gestured around him. "Like, it's a beautiful day. The sun is shining."

Judy answered the question a bit differently. "In living with dogs and training dogs, you become aware of your own capacity for making change in another living being, how well or badly you can do those things. I've learned to hold my temper, because dogs don't respond well to anger."

She recounted once taking Luca to obedience classes. The trainer asked her to do something and when Luca failed the trainer took the leash and jerked her harshly. "It just made her cower, " said Judy. "It didn't teach her anything except that he was a bad man. And if you think about it, when did harsh behaviour ever lead to anything positive?" She paused and shook her head. "I mean, just look at the world."

It would be nice to think humankind has learned that leadership is more subtle than dominance, that kindness achieves more than control, and that persuasion is more lasting than force. There is a great deal of "live-and-let-live" to observe in peaceful dog-to-animal relationships. Even among hunters and prey, constant competition and posturing isn't necessary for coexistence. There is often a kind of relaxing of rules, whereby competitors respect territorial claims. In other words, a full belly is a good political advisor.

Older dogs seem to understand this, or at least behave prudently when it comes to adversarial roles. I observed an example of this later in the summer, when I was walking the three dogs in Judy and Jeff's pasture.

I had taken to putting a bell on Tove's collar when I let him run free because it trimmed half an hour off the time required to get him back. I didn't have the bell on that morning, but he was keeping close by my side, when a big coyote came out of the bush and followed, yipping at us.

It was unusual to have a coyote at such close range— and one so vocal—but the animal didn't approach too closely, and it appeared healthy, so I suspected there was a den nearby. Sure enough, a few minutes later I spied a pup, peering from the bush. Eddie turned to investigate. The adult coyote held its ground while the pup remained visible. Eddie knew better than to allow herself to be drawn into the bush, where other coyotes might wait in ambush.

Tove, on this occasion, proved not to be much of a coyote hound after all. After rushing at the coyotes once or twice, he peeled back and stuck close to me. Luca, sensible dog that she is, wasn't interested in chasing coyotes at all. She made a bee-line for the house, and Eddie followed more slowly.

A few minutes later Eddie flopped down on the veranda and stayed there to keep watch. The adult coyote and the pup continued to study Eddie from the pasture. Eddie remained where she was for the rest of the morning, vigilant, but cool-headed, and seemed to know that it wasn't necessary to rush out to save the day.

4 HERDING DOGS

*-To use the dog as a whole dog, he must have the liberty
to use his mind-*

Jill shared her herding dog contacts with me and invited me along to her friend Arlette's sheep ranch—the better to learn about herding dogs. It was shearing day and I was part of the team that intended to relieve these woolies of their winter wear. For the first hour I was a sweeper, whipping the loose wool from around the shearers' feet and dodging the legs of the fleece sorters. Then I advanced to the position of skirter, and pulled manure tags off fleeces (butt-jewelry, we called it). I even tried my hand at throwing a fleece—the art of tossing a newly shorn fleece into the air so it lands dirty-side up, clean-side down, on the skirting frame (harder than it looks). While I worked I kept my eye on the action at the other end of the shearing shed where Jill and a handler named Jared assisted Rex, the sheepdog, to sort the sheep. I wanted to try my hand at livestock moving.

It was Rex's job to supply a steady flow of sheep to the shearing floor where Laverne, Charles and Lorrie, the stars of the operation, were hard at work. Sheep shearing is incredibly heavy work and it runs like clock-work. Each shearer selects a sheep through a set of flap doors, drags the beast about three feet to the shearing stanchion, clamps the reluctant hundred-and-seventy pounder between his legs, and then, bent at an impossible 45 degree angle (for hours), shaves the animal in a few minutes.

Watching a sheep being shorn was a bit like watching a grapefruit being peeled: a lovely naked sheep the colour of pith emerged. Once shorn, the coiffed sheep leapt up, bucked once or twice to get her bearings, and then dashed out of the shed or towards her unshorn sisters.

Meanwhile, Rex and Jared were in silent communication. Jared occasionally tossed out word or a low volume whistle. "There," "walk up," and "enough." As a livestock mover I was to help with the portable fencing. I waded out into the flock. About two hundred animals pressed around me. The sheep seemed to be experiencing what I can only describe as *group-brain*: unwilling to separate from their sisters and unwilling to change direction. I quickly worked out two basic sheep laws: 'don't be last' and 'don't be first.' Breaking either rule resulted in instant sheep chaos—which is where Rex came in.

The dog held court with the sheep in closest proximity. They gave him a wide berth and kept their eyes glued to him. Rex waited for a signal from Jared, and Jared waited for the livestock movers to make ready with the portable fencing. Once the fence sections were scissored back to receive the sheep things started to move again.

"There," said Jared, and Rex crept forward. "Away to me," and Rex flew. The sea of sheep parted.

One ornery sheep misread the situation, and instead of yielding to Rex she charged straight at him. Krak! A mid-air collision. The shock of the impact made the whole flock flinch.

Instantly, however, the sheep straightened out. Once

the fencing closed behind twenty or so sheep, Rex continued to direct them up the chute. He dove under legs, disappeared completely under a solid flank of sheep and swam his way forward. Jared whistled and Rex swam back, popping out from beneath them like a mini-submarine.

"Lie down," Jared said mildly to Rex. The dog did so at once. His desire to direct traffic was equally balanced with his desire to obey Jared. Rex held the sheep spellbound in his gaze; he might have been saying, "Go ahead and make my day," or he might have been saying, "There will be no monkey business here, ma'am." Clearly, he had no intention of enforcing the point without Jared's say-so.

Jared gave the animals a chance to calm down. A big crossways sheep had created a bottle-neck in traffic. Jared reached over the bulge of sheep with his shepherd's crook—a nativity-scene issue shepherd's staff, complete with u-shaped crook—and nudged Mrs. Crosswise. Like a cork, she popped. Once again sheep flowed up the chute.

With traffic moving steadily again towards the shearing floor the sheep settled down. The livestock movers closed gates behind every two or three animals to keep them separated in turn. The shears hummed, the wool packer growled, and the team scurried between tasks.

"Calmly, everything must be done calmly," said Jared, smiling encouragement to me. Rex flicked me a look that simply read: this is how you move sheep.

Depending on the time of year, Arlette and Allen ranch between 500 and 1000 head of sheep, including lambs and ewes. They also keep thirteen dogs, half of them herders and half guardian dogs. They started ranching about eight years ago with just *five* sheep when Arlette decided to learn something new with her border collies.

Arlette is a slightly-built young woman with a quiet,

shy manner. A dog enthusiast all her life, she was, in her own words, "consumed" by the dog world. She favored border collies and mixed-breed dogs, loved dog sports and dog rescue work, and competed in dog agility. "I didn't know just how different the world of stock dogs and livestock guardian dogs was from the rest of the dog world," she told me at their kitchen table, one spring morning.

Border collies are intense; they are all about the work. You see them in the dog park, slinking ahead of their masters and lying in wait for a ball or Frisbee; their handlers seem just as preoccupied with their demand for work. The accepted wisdom for border collies is that if you don't give them a job they'll invent one.

Which is why many border collie owners get them involved with agility and other dog sports. "Dog sports are well-suited for dogs with high drive," said Arlette, "and that's easy to get with a border collie or kelpie. If you ever attend dog sports, you'll see lots of action and lots of dogs with high drive. The intelligence is there, the intensity is there, but the purpose has shifted in dog sports."

The transition from dogs-as-pets to stock dogs and working dogs meant a major shift in paradigm for Arlette. "When you use a stock dog to move livestock," she said, "you rely on the dog's instinct as much as their energy and drive. The relationship is less about me telling the dog what to do than depending on the dog to *know* what to do."

The border collies that compete in dog sports come from the same breeders that produce working stock dogs. In fact, until fairly recently border collies were *only* bred for working with livestock. "Sport dogs haven't lost their ability to herd," said Arlette. "I guarantee the majority of them still have the instinct—it's so strong. But what they struggle with is the calmness and confidence that makes a good stock dog. A little bit of that comes from breeding, and a little bit comes from upbringing and exposure to stock."

A lot of what Arlette has learned from herding dogs has to do with trust and respect. Her first herding dog, Jayde, was a "started" border collie, meaning a dog with the rudiments of stock training. Jayde was only a year old when Arlette bought her, along with her first five sheep. Her older border collie, eleven-year-old Fynn, also followed Arlette into the sheep ranching venture, but he never achieved the confidence to become a good herder.

There are many nuances to a dog's herding style. Jayde was the one to teach her how to work livestock— how the dog uses its eye and position to move stock around. "Jayde listened to me at the beginning," Arlette said. "At least until she figured out that I didn't have a clue what I was doing."

Herding behaviour is a version of wolf hunting behaviour. Wolves often circle a herd of animals to single out individual prey. When they do this, the pack spreads out and then closes in around the prey. They often drive the prey toward a single wolf that lies in ambush.

The herding dog, never lazy, tries to play the role of several wolves at once by moving from position to position around the circle—basically acting out the roles of the whole pack. In the ambush position, the dog flattens into a kind of squat, called "clapping," and will often "give eye"—that familiar sheep dog stare that keeps sheep from breaking away from the flock.

While herding behaviour is genetically programmed in dogs, the bedrock on which training builds is the dog's desire to cooperate. As Jill had pointed out earlier, the dog wants to please you and believes the two of you are a hunting team, which is why you can send the dog out as a predator and he won't take down your stock ("If I send a Malamute out to bring me sheep," she'd added, "he'll bring me sheep all right, but they'll be dead.")

I had assumed that Tove didn't have a herding bone in his body but recently I'd seen him round up some yearling steers. We were walking along the edge of a pasture one day when he took off after them. One steer cut away from the herd and he chased back. Once he had banded the steers together in a tight little knot, Tove peeled back to me—as surprised as I was by the tidy outcome.

But herding behaviour is, after all, hunting behaviour. This unexpected move now made sense to me. The ability to control livestock has made dogs valuable to us for thousands of years. According to some historians, herding dogs may have helped to establish pastoralism, the precursor to agriculture.

Stock dogs have an attribute called "giving eye"—the tendency to watch and follow animals with their eyes. The "eye" is not unique to herding dogs. Greyhounds are superb trackers, and so are retrievers. Pointers and setters will "set" the animal of interest in the distance, but non-herding breeds are less able to keep track of large numbers of animals.

For singling out lead animals and strays, and understanding herd dynamics, the stock dog is the acknowledged expert. A herding dog stalks and sets through a combination of "eye" and "style." One style is clapping—crouching on the ground like a wolf, ready to ambush—and another is called "upstanding," or standing upright on their feet. A third characteristic, not altogether understood, is a combination of many traits, called "power." Power is simply the ability to make livestock move.

In 1945 an Australian veterinarian named R.B. Kelley categorized eye traits in sheep dogs. A "strong-eyed" dog gains control by staring the sheep down. With "over eye," the dog is so firmly fixed on an animal that he becomes immobile, like a pointer. A "medium-eyed" dog controls sheep by fixing on first one sheep and then another. "Freeeyed" dogs tend to run their eyes over the whole group instead of fixing on particular individuals. "Light-eyed" dogs might barely drop their heads to get a visual on the animal. Dogs with "no eye," which Kelley called "hoolem-up dogs," tend to use other means to get the sheep moving, like barking and rushing at them (Wall and DeMille, 1996).

The typical British border collie that we see televised in sheep-dog trials is a silent dog that shows eye, is often a clapper, and carries its tail low in a stalking posture. These dogs have the "power of eye" but the eye alone isn't what makes them successful herders. A dog can show a lot of eye and still be a weak herder. She may be reluctant to get up when called, or she may rush in and grip, or bite the sheep.

Some experts say dogs with great power tend to be upstanding dogs with moderate eye. Others contend that strong dogs are able to make sheep move simply by walking towards them. Power, Arlette believed, depends on the confidence of a dog. A powerful dog can control a stubborn ewe, or push sheep through gates and around things they are reluctant to skirt.

For the next two hours at Arlette's kitchen table she tried to teach me a thing or two about dogs and sheep. One is predator, the other, prey. Border collies and kelpies are called gathering breeds. She used the salt shaker and some napkins to set up the different herding scenarios.

For the dog to control livestock, she has to go to the head of the herd to influence their direction. To "gather," she must not only be *in* this space, but the sheep must yield to her pressure. The way sheep are gathered is different from the way cattle are driven. The stock dog, working on predatory instinct, feels the urge to move the sheep. The impulse to move animals is different from aggression.

"They will stalk, they will eye, they will come forward, and they might bring teeth into the picture," Arlette said.

"The best dogs show enough confidence and calmness to make the livestock move without thinking there is any other choice in the matter. Like, right now!"

Does aggression play a role in herding? Her feeling was that aggression was different from predatory intention. "I don't think the dogs see the sheep as adversaries. Mind you, I have seen dogs that don't like particular ewes. I've watched my kelpie be much harder on one particular ewe that has repeatedly given him trouble. There might be a level of aggression in that," she conceded.

I had read somewhere that some stockmen claimed the best sheepdog was a dog that had killed sheep. I asked her what she thought of this statement. She didn't necessarily agree, but she interpreted it like this.

"I think it means the dog is very effective, because he believes he can hunt and kill—he knows how to do it. But as shepherds, we're not going to let the dog kill. The dog doesn't know that. And as much as the dog reads the intention of the stock, the stock is reading the dog. The key is for the dog to believe that he has the power, and it's important not to take that out of the dog."

A dog who believes in himself will rarely need to use teeth because his intention is clearly understood. As Arlette put it, "That dog will have so much self-confidence that every other animal will know it too: that dog is a hunter and can kill."

A sheep's skull is thick, and if they feel threatened or cornered they will run over you or ram you. At the other extreme, a sheep might physically give up and lie down. And what's a dog to do with an animal that either charges or just isn't going to move? In those two situations a dog may grab and bite. Guardian dogs may also resort to nipping at a sick sheep to get it up and moving with the flock.

There is a lot of sugar-frosting on our ideas about herding dogs but life with stock animals isn't a Disney movie. In sheepdog trials, with a small number of sheep in a controlled environment, a dog is docked for nipping sheep. In the stock world--an uncontrolled environment where the dog is looking after hundreds or more sheep-- things play out a little differently.

Control is a relative concept with sheep dogs. Arlette made the analogy of hiring someone to do a job; she would expect them to use their tools appropriately. "A stock dog's teeth are his tools and his mind is another tool. He uses both, and the expectation is that he uses them wisely."

When you are an inexperienced handler with a dog that feels so confident that he overrides your commands, that can be pretty scary, Arlette admitted. What you then perceive is a level of uncontrolled aggression. But for her, much of the paradigm shift came from understanding the dog's innate ability. "We don't want so much obedience that it overrides the dog's instinct," she pointed out. "His instinct is what we need him for."

This was Arlette's first "aha" moment, taught to her by her friend and fellow stockman, Dave Viklund, and her first dog, Cajun, who showed her the consequence of overriding instinct. "If you over-drill a dog with obedience, you *will* override instinct. And then you'll get to a point where you *must* whistle, you *must* direct every move, because the dog has been taught that way. For my purposes, it was an error to override the dog's instinct with my obedience training. That's where the trust and respect come in."

Extrapolating from this she went on to observe that humans don't tap into their instincts very often, and it is hard for us to trust innate ability. "The truth is, we're told what to do and when to do it for almost every situation in life. We're an obedient society. But when you are working with stock, there are many unpredictable moments, and you need to rely on instinct."

She has learned to refrain from being too quick with obedience commands. If she and the dog are working 500 sheep, she can't even see the dog out in front of the flock. "So how can I be telling him to step right or step left? By the time I see what is needed, the sheep will be gone like deer."

Cooperation is one of the basic things we ask of our dogs. We *are* an obedient society. We get easily hung up on power issues. Taking direction is something border collies do very well, and is what makes them valuable to us. But bid ability may have more to do with pack communication, as Arlette pointed out, than just obeying a leader.

Pack members must know and trust that everyone is working on the same plan: the hunt. Bid ability may be more about operating with a common intention. My dog, Tove, at the other end of the biddable spectrum, was bred to run fast, which he does at every opportunity. Never is he more in his element than when he is chasing something fleet-footed. He has a one-track mind, and speed and power are his only strategies.

Hierarchy in packs, like bid ability, may have evolved to reinforce cooperation within the group. Hierarchy ensures that everyone plays an appropriate role. The "like-me, love-me" attitude of dogs is a juvenile wolf characteristic that appeals to humans, like floppy ears, short faces, and puppy looks—and their junior status enhances our position in the pack. Adult wolves, on the other hand, must continually make bold and independent decisions.

Many people, including some dog people, confuse dog obedience with dog intelligence. To illustrate the difference between pure obedience and intelligence in the field, Arlette described her kelpie's behaviour—a bit different in the bid ability department.

The kelpie is an Australian sheep dog, with a shorter coat than the border collie, resembling a cross between the German shepherd and the Doberman. Kelpies have been traditionally used to manage large flocks over long distances. At first glance, they might not seem as sharp as the border collie in terms of style and ability to take commands on-the-fly. But Arlette's kelpies have solved many problems in the field on their own.

Arlette had come to rely on her oldest kelpie, Cajun, when gathering flocks in hilly terrain. "The kelpie is a true *mustering* dog, as they'd say in Australia. If I take my border collie out to a flock of several hundred animals, she'll bring sheep all right, but the kelpie does more. After Cajun has crested the hill, found the sheep and started them moving in my direction, he'll leave that group and make his way to the next hill. He has learned that sometimes there are *more* sheep further on. So now, after we do a gather, if I ask him to do a recall, he might *not* do it. Instead, he'll go around another hill and get up on his hind feet, looking for more sheep."

Arlette smiled and paused, considering her next statement. "Instead of me thinking he's not a biddable dog, I'm thinking, 'How did he figure out there were more sheep?' How did he decide to leave one group and check for another? My border collie will be so focused on the sheep she has in front of her that she'll never check for more sheep on her own."

Many times when Arlette was sure that she had all her sheep, Cajun would indicate otherwise—and he'd be right. This has forced her to give up the notion of having to be right. "Having to be right" is a common trap for dog handlers. For her, the whole concept of right and wrong is called into question.

"Working with dogs has nothing to do with doing things correctly and everything to do with what is required in the moment. Nobody puts pressure on us to be right all the time, but somehow we believe it. It's engrained in us. If I put my dog in an obedience trial, I think, 'God, I hope he doesn't do that sloppy sit thing he's got going on.' Because that would be *wrong* to the judge. But I've had to give that up. It's just not what is required in the field."

In the dog's world, Arlette believed, the concept of right or wrong never occurs to the dog. The dog hears the command, and knows what it means, but there's something else out there that needs to be attended to. In the dog's mind, that's not wrong. "That's a hard lesson to learn for people who think obedience is important," she admitted. "Another lesson I've learned is not to take a dog's disobedience personally. I still need that 'lie down,' but now I can look around and ask, 'What else are you listening to?'"

Every day in the field is a different day and each new situation calls for a solution. For her, the bottom line is that the dog has a mind. "If you are going to use the dog as a whole dog, he needs to have a mind that is unimpaired. He needs to have the liberty to use his mind. And that *is* one piece that is very different from a pet, or an agility or fly-ball dog. Here, I need a mind who knows those sheep better than I do."

5 GUARDIAN DOGS

-Stewardship and integrity-

On a summer morning I am clinging to the frame of an all-terrain vehicle, bouncing across an alfalfa field. At the wheel is Arlette, scanning the horizon. We are on a mission to find the range guardians this morning. She yells above the wind, "I should warn you, Oakley will want to check you out, and he can be very rude about it."

Between the tearing of my eyes and the acres of rolling pasture I can hardly see the sheep, let alone the dogs. In the distance, a huge coyote-coloured dog appears, then a bear-shaped dog emerges from the terrain. One by one, the guardians materialize from the flock. In moments, the dogs are running alongside the Ranger—and can they ever move!

As soon as the vehicle stops, Oakley, a Great Pyrenees-Akbash cross, has his huge paws up on the running board. He gives me a big doggy grin and leans into me—all one hundred-and-twenty pounds of him—just to make sure we understand one another. I'm a stranger on his patch, but he reads my good intentions. Two Anatolian shepherds, brothers Whiskey and Diesel, and another Great Pyrenees-Akbash cross named Glory, soon cluster around us. A fifth guardian, Lady, a Maremma, won't approach us, but she seems happy to keep to the fringes of the greeting party.

Four of the five dogs are friendly and pet-able, in spite of the fact they have never spent much time with people. These are the wolf-descendants that literally lie down with the lambs—except on the coldest days when these ones might bed down in a shelter or a hay-filled school bus a few miles from the farmyard.

Guardians spend their whole lives with the sheep. Many sheep ranchers have sheepdogs that serve dual purposes, both to herd and to guard stock, and they will usually be more accepting of people and animals than range guardians. Range guardians will be out on pasture constantly, and the closest they'll come to human habitation is if they wander through a farmyard while on duty.

Coming from a "dogs-in-the-house" kind of background, Arlette told me that she struggled at first with leaving them outside in the extremes of winter. But, as she pointed out, it would be far unkinder to invite a dog inside for warmth and companionship and then turn him out again. The guardians' thick heavy coat, their massive feet, and their proximity to the sheep—often, literally in the midst of the flock—protect them from the cold. On the hottest days of summer they lie low when the predators are at rest.

The guardians treat the sheep as their primary unit. They also have one another for company. Arlette feeds the dogs in the field and works with them to ensure they are familiar with people as well as with her stock dogs. Guardians and herding dogs are at opposite ends of the canine behaviour spectrum: one the hunter, the other the protector.

Arlette's and Allen's land is rolling terrain with a significant coyote and raptor bird population. The need to control sheep predators is as old as shepherding itself.

Guardian dogs evolved in a time when human shepherds followed the flock, far away from human activity. Even today, guardian dogs don't work entirely alone. A combination of sound sheep management and dog handling practices are necessary to use guardian dogs successfully.

The ewes lamb in the pasture in May, unprotected by pens or enclosures. When Arlette and Allen first started ranching they learned about predator pressure the hard way, by losing lambs and yearling ewes. They tried hunting and trapping predators but wanted a more humane solution. When Arlette found her best guardian dog dead in a snare (and the coyote the dog was trailing in an adjacent snare) she vowed to find a less painful way to manage sheep, predators and dogs.

It wasn't easy to find livestock guardians in the local dog circles she moved in. Finding the right-sized working packs for their flocks was also a challenge—and this is key to using the dogs successfully, she observed. Dogs that form strong pack attachments (that is, dogs understanding pack dynamics) work more easily with unfamiliar dogs. Dogs of similar social status often have trouble getting along, and female-to-female working relationships are trickier to negotiate than females with males, or males with other male dogs.

Rearing techniques are important to produce confident and well-adjusted guardian dogs. Arlette brought up her guardian pups in a small paddock, away from the farmyard, with a few well-mannered sheep and a separate shelter for the pups. Diesel and Whisky were raised with an older dog named Willow to provide them with some leadership. The pups took their cues from Willow for their first interactions with sheep.

Arlette believes there are many misconceptions about guardian dogs. "There's an assumption that guardians know how to guard sheep, but they don't," she said. "They have the ability to form a strong sense of unit and to protect that unit. If you put them with goats, they'll bond with goats. If you put them with your toddlers, that's who they'll include in their world."

Training guardian pups is mostly a matter of exposing them to sheep during the critical eight to twelve week socialization period when pups typically bond with their primary unit. Arlette usually checked up on the pups three or four times a day in the rearing paddock. She taught them not to jump up on her, handled their ears and their feet, and showed them respect of space—meaning, "I'm here, give me some space, and I'll give you some space."

Ownership of space is a concept many animals abide by and, while guardians may not be obedient to human commands, they are very respectful of space. "*If* they respect you," she added.

When introducing the guardian pups to the larger flock Arlette takes pups out to the flock for a few hours each day, gradually lengthening the time until they can be left overnight. The pups have to get comfortable with the ewes and the ewes have to get comfortable with the pups.

Some pups, on graduating from a few sheep to several hundred sheep, are none too certain of the new environment. To build self-reliance and independence in the pack, the pups have to learn how to fit in with the other dogs as well as the sheep. Most adult dogs accept the youngsters, and fights are rare. Initially, Arlette is on hand to break up any incidents, but the dogs have to figure out their own working relationships.

As the pups mature their interactions with one another help them to forge cohesive working teams. Not every dog bonds strongly with sheep, but the dog's performance depends partly on her independent nature. The best guardians have a calming effect on the sheep, however each dog has a different style of managing sheep.

Oakley, for example, showed a lot of bravado, while Lady approached the sheep gently yet not fully at ease. Establishing good relations with the lead ewe is an important step in the introductions to the flock. Generally, the guardians chase away anything that threatens the flock. In Arlette's view, there isn't a perfect ratio of dogs to sheep—it depends on the area to be covered, predator load and pack dynamics—but more than anything finding the most effective teams depends on getting the right dogs in the right working combination.

When it comes to matching guardians, Arlette had no doubt that individual personalities matter. Diesel, for instance, was a bit of a "hot-head," assertive to the point of domineering, and more than willing to fight when provoked. Lady, his counterpart, was "cool-headed." She was a follower, but still a confident dog. Lady was more likely than Diesel to give peace a chance, so these two dogs worked well together.

Developing the guardians' relationship with the herding dogs was a different kind of challenge, one that required more careful supervision. The herding dogs, with their somewhat antagonistic role towards the sheep, can be at odds with their protectors. And since border collies and kelpies are less than half the size and weight of the guardians, the potential exists for conflict with a serious outcome.

Arlette frequently brought the herding dogs out to the field with her in order to familiarize them with the guardians. A recent incident underscored the importance of this familiarization. One morning, she let one of her young kelpies run ahead of the Ranger. She could see the sheep out ahead, and the dog was still some distance from the flock. The guardians were nowhere in sight. The kelpie was tracking, his nose to the ground, when suddenly she saw three guardians, running flat out across the field— aimed for her kelpie.

"What they saw was not a dog with *me*, but a dog running in the pasture. I drove fast! I raced those dogs for my stock dog."

Luckily, when she was close enough to call in the

stock dog, the guardians forfeited the attack. They might not have outright killed him, she surmised, but there may have been a scuffle. The guardians might have recognized the kelpie at the last second—they *had* met him several times—"*if* the adrenalin didn't carry them right into a fight."

The guardians eventually become accustomed to the herding dogs' intrusion with the flock—although, depending on the personalities involved, certain guardians might get in between the herding dog and the flock, or run the sheep together to protect their perimeter. Generally however, the herders and guardians learn to accept one another and get on with the job.

Arlette thought the guardian dogs had taught her more about the nature of dogs than any other breed. A lot of what she learned came from simply observing the dogs carry out their genetic purpose.

"It's a rare thing to watch a dog live and act out its purpose," she said. "As a pack, living without constant human interference, we can really see them be dogs."

I could not help but wonder what went into the genes of a guardian dog. Tove appeared to completely lack this trait for stewardship. There was nothing proprietary or protective about him. I suspected that if I was ever threatened, he would tuck his tail and run. As watchdogs, sighthounds are deemed more likely to "watch" thieves empty the house than to intervene.

Was bonding with the pack alone responsible for the guarding trait? Were there behavioural trade-offs for lacking the guardian disposition? Tove was getting to know his urban territory and our usual routes in the dog-park. His personal daily stake-out was my bed and the couch. Sometimes the cat would join him, and together they would watch the street from the window.

6 HUNTING DOGS

-Learn from mistakes. Care for one another.-

In an effort to show Tove that the world was a kinder place than he imagined I took him with me on errands, visiting friends, and occasionally to work. My circle of familiars was narrowing to people with dogs, or at least to people who liked and accepted my odd companion. On cool cloudy days he preferred to stay in the car, curled in the back seat, making himself as small as possible. I started to think about the demands that we place on our companion dogs. There *are* dogs bred for certain tasks *and* for companionship, but Tove wasn't one of them.

The working and companion dogs most familiar to many of us are hunting dogs. When I was a child my father had a registered German short-haired pointer named Bruni V. Wideman. She was as slim and shapely as a movie star, with liver-coloured spots on her dark brown shiny coat. In spite of her classy name, we called her Mutz. She was high-strung, an attribute that was excused on account of her good looks and her affection for my father.

Mutz and my father were inseparable. They trained continually in the backyard, in the park, in roadside fields. She responded to whistle commands and to hand signals. I still feel strong emotion at the sight of a canvas training dummy; it brings her back to me instantly.

Every autumn the greatest privilege of my ten-year-old world was to accompany my father and Mutz on a duck-hunting trip. I wasn't a fan of the noise and the smell of gunpowder, or those inert little bodies we had to clean at the end of the day, but I loved the hunt: the crisp fall day, hunkered down in the slough grass, staring up at the sky. We were always perfectly silent in the field—at least until Mutz did something wrong-headed. Then, there'd be an abrupt screech of the whistle and my father's thunderous commands. Mostly, however, we were quiet as we waited, united in purpose. To me, the essence of the hunt was in this wordless communication.

I caught up with Joe at Sunnynook Kennels on a different kind of fall day, one that threatened snow. Catching Joe and his hunting dogs at home on a Sunday during hunting season was lucky indeed. Joe, a burly bearded German-Canadian, was in the yard doing a demonstration with Fauna, one of his Large Munsterlanders. A fellow-hunter had stopped by to observe the exercise; he was considering getting a puppy from next year's Sunnynook litter.

Fauna trotted quietly at heel beside Joe until they reached the end of the acreage driveway. The dog was calm and precise in her movements and scanned the bush ahead. She began to range in the tall grass, head cocked, eyes bright. She glanced from time to time towards Joe, seeming to expect a word or signal from him. I recognized, in that silent split-second exchange between them, the same understanding that used to pass between my father and Mutz.

When Fauna heard the rustle of wings she halted abruptly; she was directly downwind from a pigeon trap that Joe had planted at the foot of the driveway. Instantly, she locked into point. She didn't move a hair. It was an absolute stillness that resembled paralysis.

I had joined the hunter near the garage to watch the demonstration. Tove was in the car. I could see Tove watching Fauna with rapt attention. "How long will she hold it?" the hunter asked Joe. "Oh, she'll stand like that for five minutes," Joe said quietly. "Then she might sit down."

After about a minute Joe sprang the pigeon trap by remote-control and the bird soared up and flew back towards the house. Still, Fauna didn't move. Had the pigeon been the genuine quarry, she would have stood for the shot and waited for a signal from Joe to retrieve the bird. Fauna passed the test again and again.

I checked on Tove in the car—he was comfortably napping. Minutes later, Joe and I were toweling off muddy bellies and paws on the back porch of the house, a half a dozen wet Large Munsterlanders roiling around us. With that task done, we went into the living room where Sheila, Joe's wife and partner in Sunnynook Kennels, was finishing up negotiations with the hunter.

A cheery fire crackled in the fireplace and the dogs cozied up next to us. Soon we each had a dog or two in our laps (they politely kept their back feet on the floor). Fauna settled beside me, pressing her silky black and white flanks against my legs. I was instantly smitten with her.

Large Munsterlanders, affectionately known as LMs in bird dog circles, are the German superstars of hunters, and Joe and Sheila are serious LM breeders. The couple was recommended to me by a friend. Joe is a biologist who is well known in upland game hunting circles. He also writes about LMs, which are known as versatile hunters, meaning they both point and retrieve.

"When you think about it, retrieving and pointing are opposite intentions," he said. "Pointing requires exaggerated stillness—the 'wait-before-the-pounce move' in the wild—and retrieving requires chasing, catching and returning the bird—just the opposite of standing still."

Breeding for hunting performance and traits like

cooperativeness, perseverance and trainability, is an exacting science, and Joe and Sheila have been breeding LMs for thirty years. Sheila is a geneticist. She and Joe are active in wildlife conservation. When I asked Joe why he preferred LMs to other hunting breeds he said the LM's intelligence and temperament are a cut above others.

In Germany, where Joe grew up, hunting required both a license and a hunting area lease. If you didn't have the good fortune to inherit a hunting area lease, and were determined to hunt upland birds, the best way to improve your chances of being invited to hunt was to have a hunting dog. Joe's uncle helped him to get his first LM puppy. When Joe immigrated to Canada he wasn't able bring the dog with him. By the time Joe and Sheila married and returned to Germany for their honeymoon, the dog was too old to be uprooted from his uncle's place, so Joe and Sheila spent the rest of their honeymoon looking for an LM puppy. That puppy was Amsel vom Siegerland, who came back to Canada in a bread basket as carry-on luggage. Amsel became the dam of a long line of Sunnynook LMs. Sheila pointed to the original bread basket, which now held kindling on the hearth.

A dip into the dog literature told me the history of hunting dogs mirrors the history of human hunting weapons—from the running of hounds in the spear-throwing days to the flushing of birds in the shotgun era. All dogs do more or less what their ancestors, the wolves, have evolved to do: nurture families, cooperate as a social group and hunt. While all dogs perform hunting behaviours, some breeds are better at it than others and some specialize in more than one technique. The versatile breeds like the LM, in Joe's view, bring all the hunting skills to bear most consistently: locating, waiting, retrieving, and returning with the quarry.

Fauna, for example, not only pointed at the quarry, but she held the position for long enough for Joe to stalk, flush the bird, aim, and hit it with his single shot. The successful training of a bird dog, according to Joe, is the result of asking the dog to do what she is intended to do, genetically speaking.

Gun dogs include spaniels, setters, retrievers and pointers. Besides having the physical attributes to suit different terrain, each breed specializes in one or more type of hunting. Spaniels, sometimes called springers, are built for dense undergrowth and moving along slough margins. They cast around for scent or movement and run out in front of the hunter. "Basically they just flush the bird out, without any warning," said Joe.

Retrievers are taller so they are better suited to long grass and reeds and for spotting where the birds fall. Because they love water they excel at hunting water fowl. When retrievers bring back uneaten game they are doing a variation of the wolf's cooperative behaviour of carrying back food to the den for the pups.

Pointers and setters look directly at the spot where the game is located, just like the wolf spots and focuses on its prey. "Each breed has its particular strength," Joe said, "and there are, of course, exceptional individuals in every breed."

Hunting behaviours are evident in LM puppies from an early age. Joe used the "wing-on-a-stick" method to test the pups' hunting aptitudes. This involved dangling a bird wing on a string in front of the puppy to observe its reaction. "It usually takes very little to engage the pointing behaviours," he said. Sheila added that there is a period of time when, with minimal training, you can get quite high pointing scores from puppies. "And then the pup goes through the terrible teens," she said, "and if you test your dog during the terrible teens…. Teenagers will challenge."

Joe and Sheila presently had three eligible breeding females. They kept a waiting list of people who wanted their pups, and didn't breed their dogs unless they had several prospective buyers. Being last on the list didn't necessarily mean you wouldn't get a puppy that year.

"People's circumstances change," Sheila acknowledged. "Some breeders take deposits, some try complicated contracts. We don't do that. The worst thing that can happen is that you take a puppy when you're not ready."

Did they screen prospective owners? Yes and no. "Some jokingly accuse us of running an elite puppy placement agency, the way we question prospective owners," Sheila laughed. "But, no, we don't necessarily know the people who want the pups." "We want the dogs to go to hunters," Joe emphasized. "Given their drive and intensity, LMs are happiest when they are hunting. I always say if you're just an occasional weekend hunter, you don't want an LM. Get a retriever."

We talked briefly about the role of personality in successfully homing pups. Sheila shook her head. "Puppies are still malleable. These guys," she pointed to the dogs at our feet, "yes, I could describe each personality." Joe countered that certain personality traits *were* obvious in young pups, but Sheila argued that personality was adaptable in pups. Personality, she believed, is heavily influenced by environment and upbringing. "By the time a dog is older and personality is more developed, finding the right home for any dog will be more difficult."

It may be more accurate to say that certain tendencies can be observed in very young pups. Joe thought these tendencies *become* part of the dog's personality. "The demeanor of a puppy is part of its personality. Persistence and drive are part of personality. How far away pups want to be from you, how long they want to stay with you, who comes out of the kennel first—these things are often quite telling."

He went on to say that hunters sometimes look for certain traits in pups. On one occasion, he recalled, a pup had gone off on its own to explore, while all the others stayed together. "That pup was independent enough to be on his own," Joe said, "and the buyer said, 'I like that.'"

The hunter who had visited Sunnynook that day, the

prospective buyer, was a former police dog handler, and he wanted to assess the puppies at a certain stage and to base his choice on the result of that assessment. "We can do that," Joe said. Sheila said they encouraged new owners to name the puppy before they picked it up. They also liked to send pictures of the pup as it developed—just to help foster that future bond. "We always hope the right pup will be the one that comes forward," she said. "But first impressions can be deceiving."

Joe pointed out that purebred LMs have been selected for certain behaviours for over a hundred years, so there is uniformity in their characteristics. Joe and Sheila were both strong proponents of purebred dogs, an unpopular stance in dog culture these days, according to Sheila. Personally, she felt that if someone wanted a certain set of characteristics they should be able to pick a breed and know there is a high probability of getting those traits. "Purebreds denote there will be a narrower gene pool, and that, from a breeder's point of view, is a good thing."

When I asked about the importance of genetic diversity to animal health, she pointed out that adaptability wasn't nearly as important in an animal that was fed and cared for. "There are about three hundred breeds of dogs today, so across the breeds there's lots of diversity. The cult of diversity is highly overdone in domestic animals. Ideally, a domesticated animal should be homozygous for all the traits that you want. You want no diversity. That's the irony of it."

Not that inbreeding isn't a concern to breeders. Joe and Sheila guaranteed sound hunting dogs from their puppies but they did not guarantee breeding stock. Good breeding, Joe claimed, was one the hardest thing he'd ever done. Like most good breeders, Joe and Sheila travelled long distances to find suitable mates for their dogs. They x-rayed every dog for hip dysplasia, and Joe watched the dogs closely for signs of potentially inheritable flaws.

He showed me Fauna's pedigree and explained the

meaning of the computation of inbreeding coefficient, a measurement of the degree of inbreeding. The coefficient is based on both parents' pedigrees, and is calculated over five generations. A grandfather-to-granddaughter mating yields a score of 12.5, cousin-to-cousin, 6.3. The pups in Fauna's present litter had a coefficient of 0, so she had no ancestors in common in a five generation pedigree.

"We certainly pay attention to genetics," Joe said, "but if diversity was our goal we'd breed our dogs to the coyote—and lose the benefit of a hundred years of selection."

It is true that the coyote needs more versatility to survive than Fauna. The fact that Fauna was a really good pointer doesn't necessarily mean that as a feral dog she wouldn't starve—we don't know that for sure, Joe pointed out. She was highly intelligent, and intelligence was one trait genetically selected for over many generations. And for Joe, intelligence really was the exceptional characteristic of LMs. "When people say that this is a really intelligent breed the scientist in me asks, 'What's the evidence?'"

Intelligence in dogs has been difficult to measure because so much depends on the dog's motivation during testing. Some scientists argue against trying to measure mental ability in animals at all because we are limited to our own species-specific interpretation of intelligence. Behaviourists see animal behaviour in terms of response to stimuli, and not as the result of reasoning. Behaviourists break all behaviour into a series of responses to separate stimuli.

Joe told me about a friend of his, an animal behaviourist, who had an LM named Huchen. Huchen liked to bury every bone he was given, straight away in the garden. In an effort to keep bones around the house for a few days, Huchen was not permitted to take bones outside into the yard. One night Huchen went to the basement to find his owner and whined to be let outside. His owner followed the dog upstairs to let him out. Just before he opened the door he noticed a bone sitting directly beside the door—not the usual place for Huchen to leave his bones. As he opened it the dog made a grab for the bone. Huchen had clearly concocted a plan.

"My friend said to me, 'They aren't supposed to be able to think ahead, to plan.'" Joe chuckled. "You see, as a behaviourist, he followed Morgan's Canon, which says we shouldn't interpret the actions of an animal at any higher level than is absolutely required. That means you shouldn't interpret anything beyond what you need in order to explain the behaviour. And my friend was a very good scientist. But I think Huchen opened his eyes in terms of his views on animal behaviour."

To attribute to an animal the emotions and perceptions of a human is considered a major *faux pas* in the scientific world. The ability to plan for the future, to be self-aware and to anticipate events—these are supposedly criteria for human intelligence, a definition that has repeatedly failed to apply exclusively to humans.

Problem-solving requires not only the ability to hold a sequence of steps in mind, but remembering former strategies that have worked—old information that can be applied to the present situation. What Huchen demonstrated with his bone was pure and simple problem-solving.

What *every* dog does *every* day requires both an observant and reflective mind. At the most menial level, a dog's problem-solving requires anticipating what the human will expect of him today. Joe pointed out that intelligence and trainability are separate concepts. Joe made training a part of everyday life. "A lot of hunters train all summer in order to be ready for hunting season in the fall," he said. In his view obedience should be built into routine activities.

The bond between dog and owner will strongly influence the dog's cooperation. Fauna's drive may be part of her genetic make up, but her devotion to Joe was just as important. "They really *do* want to do it right," he said. "If Fauna finds a bird and she can't hold it, she feels so bad. I don't need to chastise her. I know that she tried her level best."

Joe has written about the ingredients that go into a good hunting dog. He noted three motivational states: desire, cooperation and obedience. The desire to hunt is inborn, as is cooperativeness in large measure. But dogs can differ in these characteristics, depending on upbringing and genetics. A trainer can easily damage the cooperative nature of the dog by using poor training methods.

Too much discipline dampens the dog's hunting desire. Joe believed the good trainer let desire motivate the seeking behaviour, cooperation prompt the return of the quarry, and obedience do the rest of the job. Many dogs seem to shift modes during different stages of the hunt. Obedience appears to be inversely proportional to the dog's distance from the hunter, and this can be a problem in the field.

"There seems to be a magical ten to fifteen yards from the hunter when the dog shifts more easily into the obedience mode. This is sometimes signaled by the dog dropping the bird and then picking it up again to complete the delivery. And it doesn't seem to be a matter of refreshing her grip, either."

On the subject of training methods, Joe used punitive methods sparingly. He didn't, however, believe a dog with the high drive of an LM could be trained with positive reinforcement alone. "As a minimum we use leash work, and if the dog chases something, she jerks herself at the end of the leash, and that's punishment. We have the electric shock collar, the e-collar, for the final training stages, to polish them in terms of steadiness. It's demanding to stand on point, to stand for the shot, and to wait until I tell her to fetch. Some dogs are even, some are variable. They don't need to experience the e-collar more than once or twice. It's for training only. Generally, if you need to hunt with an e-collar, you've not done the job right."

When I asked him what he had learned from the dogs he was thoughtful for a moment. "A lot of hunters yell and use the whistle the whole time. Personally, I just decided I'm not going to yell. They need to make mistakes. They learn from mistakes, if they're interested in doing it right. We all learn from our mistakes."

Fauna had fallen asleep beside me. Her head rested lightly on my foot. The youngster of the pack, Zeni, was nibbling on a floor cushion. I asked Sheila what she had learned from the dogs. At first she said she wasn't good at that kind of introspection, but then, "I think the most interesting thing I've learned comes from observing the pack and all their little interactions. In this pack, I'm the midwife, and I develop a real bond with the girls when they whelp. Lots of them have their puppies almost in my lap. I spend the night on the floor with them. I also watch how they take care of each other. Sometimes we miss an injury on a dog. We see one or two of the dogs get up and lick at another dog. I'll take a closer look and find a cut there. The dogs have noticed it first, and sometimes it's in a place on the dog where she can't reach. I'm fascinated by the level of care they give to each other in the pack."

Given more time to reflect, Joe later observed of his hunting relationship with Fauna, "It's very humbling in a way. When we are out there together, more often than not, I see a purposeful cooperation in the way she works with me. She has the hunting desire, and even the desire to grab the bird, but she's learned to keep that under control to ensure that we, jointly, are successful. One might say she is simply acting out a thousand-year-old selection process for cooperative behaviour—or a hundred-year-old process for this particular breed. But I think it's more than that. There is a connection that happens that somewhat blurs the distinction between human and animal."

7 POLICE DOGS

-Perseverance and trust-

I am crouched between two police cars where Sergeant Lorne has placed me for safety. I've never been afraid of dogs—never felt the need to feel fearful—but the wild barking from inside the police cars is making me sweat under my parka. A heavyset man weaves across a snowy parking lot toward Constable Kelly, who stands a dozen yards away from us. Kelly's dog, Baron, is shut up in the back of one of the cars. The police cars literally rock with barking dogs.

What I don't know at this moment is that officers can release their dog remotely from a patrol car. When Constable Kelly does just that the sedan's back door springs open and one hundred pounds of German shepherd launches out like a missile. In less than a second, the dog registers his handler and the man who is stalking him. Kelly momentarily calls him off and Baron drops to the ground, as motionless as a stopped-action film-frame—and then, on Kelly's signal, he explodes forward again.

I wince as Baron slams into the stalker and drags him in a half circle. The stalker—rather, the man pretending to stalk Constable Kelly and who is playing the quarry today—is Constable Eddie, and Baron knows this exercise. After a few moments of intense drag-out-haul-down action the constable slips from the training sleeve and a triumphant Baron dances away with the trophy arm-pad.

The three officers and I cheer to let the dog know he's done his job. It's a light-hearted moment, a snapshot of the affection and camaraderie, that the policemen share with their dogs.

On a bright snowy January morning I met up with Sergeant Lorne and the two other handlers for this demonstration. The hunter I'd met at Joe and Sheila's had recommended Sargent Lorne to me. Sergeant Lorne, a seasoned officer with a friendly smile, introduced me to the two younger officers. He also introduced me to Duncan, a gangly three-month-old pure black German shepherd.

Police dogs usually start training between thirteen and eighteen months of age so Duncan was unusual on several counts. First, he came from a German shepherd breeder in Saskatchewan, not a service dog breeder, and second, he was part of an experiment to see if the Police K-9 Section could produce a better police dog by having him follow the officers for a year before his formal training began.

Police dogs come from all over the world—and they don't come cheap. Lorne's dog, Jet, was from the United States; Kelly's dog, Baron, from the RCMP kennels in Alberta; and Eddie's dog, Kato, from Holland. Each untrained dog cost the equivalent of a couple of months of an average officer's take-home pay, and they are usually purchased by law-enforcement agencies from breeders of service dogs.

Lorne had been with the K-9 Section of our local police services for more than a dozen years and had trained five police dogs. Duncan was in experienced hands, but that was no guarantee the pup would make the grade. He would have to pass many tests over the next year. Lorne said Duncan showed early promise when he was first tested.

"We take the dogs everywhere our jobs take us," he said. "We immerse them in everything—places with tile floors, open-grate stairs, malls with lots of people. If they show reluctance for certain tasks or environments we can work on that, but if they can't get past it we have to find a different dog."

By the time Duncan was trained he would be worth between fifty and sixty thousand dollars in training hours alone. Duncan's life as a police dog would be, in many ways, a privileged one. He would go where other dogs don't normally follow, and be with his handler 24-7. He would enjoy a high work value, but the job came with risks. His life would depend on his handler's judgment, as his handler's life might someday depend upon him. He might be injured in the line of duty. Plus he would work harder each week than most dogs work in a lifetime.

There is no doubt that police dogs have remarkable skills: they detect things we can't detect, they apprehend armed criminals and protect law enforcement officers. Few would dispute the contribution to society these dogs make. But is it just their training that makes them valuable to us?

Clearly, there is more to the relationship than the tasks they perform. I asked why some breeds were more highly valued for this line of work than others. Not every dog can be trained in criminal apprehension, scent tracking, and officer protection, plus one other specialty. Lorne's goal for the K-9 Section was to have each of their nine dogs trained in a specialty as well as in general duties. Kelly's dog, Baron, for example, was trained in drug detection, and another dog in the Section was trained to detect explosives. Other breeds can be trained to do a piece of what Duncan will do someday, but in Lorne's opinion, German shepherds are the best overall dog for police work.

"They're not the best tracking dog in the world," he said, "they've not got the best grip—pit bulls have extreme strength—but they are geared for our winters, and can work through extreme heat and cold. I've seen Rottweilers work, I've seen the Dutch shepherds work, I've seen the giant schnauzer work, and in my view the shepherd is the best all-around dog."

On reading up on police dogs I learned that German shepherds and Dutch shepherds are the preferred breeds for general police dog work in Canada. Other breeds may be used for general detection, border control, airport security, and search and rescue. Male dogs are often chosen for their strength and drive, but female dogs also serve. General police dog duties include locating lost persons, tracking criminals, finding crime-scene evidence, VIP protection and crowd control. Dogs can be trained to detect everything from drugs and currency, to bedbugs and human semen. The dogs selected must have an even temperament, good hunting instinct and sound character. They must learn to apprehend a resisting and sometimes dangerous person on command. Dogs showing reluctance to perform any of these tasks are not commissioned. Less than twenty percent of dogs entering the RCMP police dog training program, for example, graduate to service.

In elaborating on what makes shepherds ideal for police work the literature reiterated what Lorne told me: their versatility, strength and courage are their most valuable attributes. In addition, as the website for the famed RCMP police dog training program states: these dogs have "an inhibitive psychological effect on potential wrongdoers." A few more facts of interest: a police dog can search a car in three minutes. Dogs work up to four hours with rest intervals. On average, a service dog will retire at the age of seven—the equivalent to fifty-something in human years, close to the average retirement age for police officers.

Duncan was a bit sleepy, having just woken from a nap in the back of the police car. The pup appeared to be quite calm for a youngster. Lorne said he was hoping for a bit more of that explosive energy that is more typical of police dog material. He cheerfully wound Duncan up for a game of tug-of-war—holding him back on the leash and then urging him forward. Duncan grabbed the decoy dummy and bucked backwards, tugging gamely, and after a brief tussle Lorne let the pup win. The dog must always win, he told me, because it helps to build their confidence.

Jet, Lorne's eight-year-old dog, also a pure black German shepherd, was next up for a demonstration. Jet was the genuine article, and as Lorne ran him through a series of commands, Jet responded with impressive swiftness. The dog paid rapt attention to his handler and the other officers watched the performance with frank admiration. Seeing Jet in action gave me a new appreciation for obedience commands.

I couldn't help but compare him to Tove, who would have considered each command, tried to judge my seriousness, weighed the potential reward, and finally decided he was bored. Intelligence may be a relative thing, but Jet, reading Lorne's every whisper, was in a different class altogether.

The shepherd's intelligence is regarded as one of the top qualifications for the job. German shepherds are usually rated among the top three smartest breeds by dog experts. The other officers agreed that shepherds tune in quickly. Kelly said he had owned other smart dogs, including retrievers. "Both my police dogs have been ten times any dog I've ever had. I've put more training into them, sure, but the stuff these guys pick up on is incredible. It amazes me how they can find someone hiding on the roof, or in a tree. How would you *ever* find that person without them? Every day they amaze me."

The dog wears a harness when tracking and, over time, learns that when the tracking equipment comes out he is going to work. The dog will be excited and ready to go. Lorne told me that some dogs show this readiness when the handler reaches for the radio microphone or when the car picks up speed.

"We select dogs with high energy and high drive, and they form a strong bond with us. The drive they have, combined with the bond we make with them, gets stronger and stronger, until they become very good at what they do."

Importantly, police dogs are also used in community relations. Eddie told me that, depending on the circumstances, you might not know these dogs are police dogs. The officers and their dogs sometimes visit schools. "The kids will be pulling at their tails and their ears—no problem. They're very social. They like being around people, they like the attention from people. They know they're not working because we're not giving them any commands. Under these circumstances they're very relaxed. But if someone were to start yelling aggressively, they'd know that's not normal behaviour, and they'd look to the handler to find out what they should be doing. The next minute, they could be chasing somebody down an alley."

Kelly likened the shepherd's ability to shift gears to having an internal switch. The dogs are very good at reading human intention. As for distinguishing between the good guys and the bad, that also seems fairly clear to them. "If a bad person is approaching us, *we* give off certain vibes. We tense up, and the dog reads that. It all depends on how *you* react to *us*."

Policemen are good at reading body language too. For me, the question remained, how much of a dog's reaction is based on its own assessment of the situation, and how much on the handler's interpretation? Lorne said that dogs are less likely to misjudge individuals. "Dogs don't know prejudices," he said. "For them, a bad person is a bad person. We have no idea who people are when they approach us. By and large, when we're tracking someone, we don't know who we're going to catch. Our dogs don't seem to care. They just go."

He pointed out that a dog giving chase is simply responding to stimuli: the quarry flees and the chase instinct is triggered; the quarry threatens his master and the protective instinct is activated. Passive, non-threatening or non-evasive human activity—what a policeman might interpret as good behaviour—the dog sees in neutral terms. Eddie suggested that the dog sees criminal behaviour as a deviant from the norm—something that draws the attention of the hunter or protector.

I asked about fear: can dogs smell fear? Lorne said he didn't believe in the fear-scent theory. "I believe when someone is scared they may sweat more, which is what we're tracking—the disturbance of the ground combined with human skin cells falling off. Are there more skin cells falling from someone who is scared, who is running away? I don't know."

Most living creatures, from ants to bison, communicate at some level through scent. Anyone who has ever walked a dog knows that a dog's mark carries a lot of information. There is news on every surface: the age of the passing animal, sex, sexual readiness, general health and emotional state. The scent-detecting part of a dog's brain is about four times the size of the human's, and even among dogs not all noses are created equally. The German shepherd has no more scent receptor cells than the poodle, and nowhere near as many as the bloodhound.

The dog's skill as a tracker depends on his ability to separate scents—to ignore some scents and focus on others. Dogs can detect substances in minute quantities, including things buried or concealed underwater and substances diluted by space and time. When following a scent trail the dog is following human skin cells that are sloughed off in micro-sized cell rafts. The dog will note disturbances in the ground vegetation, or whatever has been stirred up as someone passed.

Given the dog's smell acuity, it seemed to me that some subtle shift in human chemistry might produce an odour. Could not adrenaline, the "fight or flight" response, trigger a highly specific odour? One would think there would be more empirical evidence, but a fear scent—hormone, pheromone or other—has never been identified in humans. The scent of fear remains a theory. Researchers conclude that it is more accurate to say that a dog 'senses' fear rather than smells it, in the same way humans sense fear, by observing body language—stiffening up, changing posture, looking directly at something.

Police dogs are, of course, more than highly trained instruments. The officers talked easily about each of their dogs' personalities. Jet was happy-go-lucky; Baron continually tried to show up his trainer; Kato enjoyed the company of the family dogs. I asked about how important it was to match the right dog to the right officer. Lorne said, "The last training round we did, we had a dog that was very outgoing, a very strong willed and powerful dog, and I tried to match him with the quieter of the two officers, hoping that the quietness of the one would balance out the strength of the other. It was a best guess. Is that done as a rule? Lots of times we don't have that luxury. Maybe we only have one position and one dog, so there's the match right there."

The officers focus on training for a part of each day. A basic training task like scent tracking usually involves taking a walk for four or five blocks to let the dogs track the quarry. One of the training techniques used is called imprinting, where the trainer drops a piece of food in his footsteps and encourages the dog to follow to get the reward. Another technique is master tracking, where a dog tracks his master with another officer. "My dog loves me, so he wants to find me quick, and we use that as incentive," Kelly said. "But we get away from that pretty soon, because I'll be tracking *with* my dog."

Duncan had been romping playfully in the snow with a scattered puppy-like kind of attention. He seemed an unlikely candidate for the tough requirements of his trade. It was hard to imagine him apprehending someone on command or to protect his master. "They're trained to hold on," said Kelly, "not to keep biting different body parts, but to grip as hard as they can, and hold on until we get there and can take the person safely into custody."

Generally, people *are* wary and inhibited by police dogs. "There are tense situations out there for our officers sometimes," said Kelly, "and when we roll up in our cars and our dogs start barking, people just disperse."

I asked Lorne how often the dogs are successful in tracking down a criminal. "We have so much working against us when we're out there," he admitted. "A person can climb into a vehicle, they can take off on a bicycle, they can go into an apartment building, a store, a mall. Time is an important factor, and so is the environment. Wind, heat and extreme cold can make the scent dissipate quickly. If someone walks where the bad guy walked and then turns, there's a cross track. All these things work against making a successful apprehension."

Kelly added, "We don't always catch the guy, but my dog always tracks him as far as the track takes us. We track to where the bike tracks appear, or the peel-out marks of car tires appear. My dog has done all he can to find where that bad guy was last."

Kelly was a tall young man with a broad smile. He struck me as a cheerful out-going sort of officer. He described his dog, Baron, as generally a happy dog, but with "a bit of an edge." "He likes to think he could be the boss one day," he said, "so he challenges me. He's strong willed. His biggest joy is coming to work and doing what he does. He's born to do it."

When I asked him what his dog had taught him, he answered without hesitation: "Perseverance. No matter how cold it is, no matter how far he has run or how many fences he has jumped, he just wants to keep going after the bad guy. At one time in my career I might have said, "I'm frozen, I'm tired, I'm soaked in sweat and covered in snow, and I'm giving up because it's not that important for me to get that guy.' But he doesn't think so. He's just *go, go, go*. So where he goes, I go. "

I changed my question slightly for Lorne, asking what the dogs had taught him about himself. Lorne thought about the question. "To trust, comes to mind," he said. "There are lots of times, especially early on in my career— probably still now, and these guys will attest to this—when I think I know where the bad guy went. But you have to trust your dog, because the dog doesn't lie. I've never seen a police dog lie. If the dog tells you that the person is over here, that's where he is. There are numerous times when I've had to admit that my dog was right, that I'd missed the track. I'd go back later and, yes, absolutely, the dog was right and I was wrong. That's happened to every one of us. Trust is a pretty big thing."

Eddie chose his answer to the question carefully. He was the quietest of the three officers, and his answers were more measured. His said that his first police dog had been "all about the work," and he hadn't been much of a cuddler—quite different from Kato, who was a more social dog. "My dog is more loyal than any person I've come across," said Eddie. "I trust my dog."

Policemen don't always come across as the most trusting individuals but the trust they place in their dogs and their fellow officers is noteworthy. Trust is a basic understanding independent of verbal exchange. Trust is perhaps what we most value in our dogs and in the individuals we choose to include in our lives.

Though we bring a lot of who we are to the picture of trust, this seems to be the one great human goal: to live and work alongside a trusted companion. That we sometimes fail our dogs and one another in the trust that is placed in us is an unfortunate truth. Police are given an inordinate amount of trust in our society and, likewise, the K-9 officers must depend on their dogs.

What happens when a police dog-in-training fails in trust? Lorne told me that a dog in training fails when he does not show progress in learning. "We picked up a young dog this summer, and the dog showed great promise. He did really well. But we have since identified that the dog has an aversion to children. We have worked on it, and we could make it better one day, but then on the following day we'd be right back to square one. We weren't seeing a distinct learning curve. If something is difficult the first time, is the second time any better? If he's better each time, we can work on that; he shows that he's learning. But this particular dog was showing continued avoidance, which is something we can't accept."

Sometimes judgments need to be quick and in black and white because the stakes for trust are very high. The police dogs that are selected for duty give years of faithful service. One day, however, even the best dogs must retire.

Police dog handlers are given the option to buy their dog from the law enforcement agency for the sum of one dollar, Lorne told me. "They're pretty tired dogs by the time they retire. I purchased my second dog and had him at home with my other police dog. It took some time for him to understand that the work was over. He'd be excited when I got up in the morning, he'd be sitting in his kennel, barking and ready to go. It took a while for him to be content with just staying home. He eventually became a house dog, and he was completely fine with it."

It was time for Duncan and the other dogs to return to the police cars, and for the officers to get back to work. In the coming days, Lorne and the other officers in the K-9 Section would do their best to see that Duncan succeeded and became an officer's trusted partner. But if that didn't happen, I had no doubt that Duncan would become someone's lifelong valued and trusted companion.

***

The importance of mutual trust was brought home to me soon after this by a more mundane incidence involving a leash and a lawn chair. Tove and I were visiting friends at their cabin, and I had hooked Tove's leash to the arm of the lawn chair as we sat outside enjoying the sun. I got up to open the porch door and Tove jumped up to follow. The lawn chair toppled and snapped shut behind him. He took off like a hound chased by the devil.

Dog and lawn chair tore around the cabin, crashing and bouncing from obstacle to obstacle. Too frantic to heed my call, he finally dove beneath the cabin and wedged himself against the footings. He could have as easily disappeared into the forest, and seriously injured himself.

I crawled under the cabin. He crouched there, shivering, as I tried to free him. I stroked him, trying to calm him. Eventually I managed to extricate him. For the rest of our stay at the cabin he looked at me warily, and with much more attention.

I had by this time gained some of his trust, but I understood that trust was still fragile. Gaining more of *his* trust would mean giving him more of *mine*. Who would be first to truly let down our guard?

8 DETECTION DOGS

-Confidence and drive build on a strong personal bond-

Winter snow turns the roads through the game preserves into broad white corridors. The wildlife use these corridors for their own highways—which makes the roads perfect for poachers. Conservation Officer Jamie and his Belgian Malinois, Jaks, are on their way east from Prince Albert to look for poaching evidence. The shooting of a bull moose was reported on the TIP line (Turn In Poachers) early this morning. Rifle shots and a spotlight were seen on the road around midnight.

With only one conservation dog team to serve the entire province, Jamie and Jaks spend a lot of time on the road. It is important to get to the site before other vehicles disturb the area. About fifteen minutes before reaching the game preserve Jamie stops the truck and plants a spent shotgun shell in the bush by the side of the road. If Jaks doesn't make a successful find today he will stop on the way back to let the dog retrieve the planted shell. It is important for Jaks to end the day with a success, to keep him feeling positive about the job.

The field officers are already at the site of the shooting. A pile of moose entrails and a disturbed area of mud and blood show where the animal was dragged. The field officers think the poachers probably winched the partially gutted moose into a truck. Finding evidence will be like looking for a needle in a haystack; at this time of year there are hundreds of game carcasses hanging in hundreds of hunters' garages—legally shot ones from legally drawn lots with purchased licenses. License isn't the issue here. Hunting at night in a game preserve close to occupied buildings is not only illegal, but dangerous.

Jamie hopes his colleagues have a suspect in mind, a repeat offender or at least a partial license plate to go on. The sale of wild game makes poaching profitable. The carcass might already have changed hands. Forensic evidence can do only so much; finding the shell casings might help to obtain a search warrant, one piece of the puzzle, but not enough for a conviction. Jamie rolls down the truck window to check the direction of the wind and then continues further down the road, beyond the disturbed area. They will work their way back on foot, facing into the wind.

He gets out of the truck and slips the search collar onto the dog. "Find it," he tells Jaks. The dog bolts ahead. Jaks isn't the kind of dog to wait for commands. One day the dog will forget his brain in the truck, Jamie thinks. His first dog, Keela, was more likely to leave her legs in the truck. She'd get out and stretch and yawn before she was ready to work.

Jaks is already twenty feet ahead of him, patterning back and forth in the snowy ditch. Jamie slides behind him at the end of the leash along the soggy road margin. In no time, he is as wet and caked with mud as the dog.

This is how the search for firearms evidence always begins, with the two of them working alone. The spent rifle cartridges may have been displaced by a passing vehicle. The poachers may have shot from the vehicle window and taken the evidence away with them. Without the dog, it would be virtually impossible to find any evidence. Jaks keeps looking back to see if Jamie will give him any clues. He has learned that he'll finds more "hides" if he pays attention to Jamie's directions.

Jamie is an athletic-looking man of indeterminate years, rugged and tanned, and he knows how to tell a story. It was the outdoor life, not dog handling, that drew him to work for the Ministry of Environment. When he finished college he became a conservation officer. He'd had dogs as a kid but he wasn't an expert handler before joining the Enforcement and Investigations Branch of the Ministry.

Wildlife conservation agencies use dogs to track poachers, to find contraband game, and locate illegal netting and game operations. A conservation dog team can check a camper trailer for illegal fish in a couple minutes— hardly holding up holiday traffic at all, compared to a manual vehicle search. Dogs have also been used for unique conservation missions surveying for species-at-risk.

Game wardens, like the police, have a long history of using canine search evidence in court. In 1940, the RCMP were the first law enforcement agency in Canada to win a court case using dog search evidence. While dog-tracking evidence is admissible in court, case law has been challenged from time to time. As Jamie pointed out, a dog is not like an instrument that can be calibrated and read by anyone. The admissibility of legal evidence from a dog— whether related to poaching or to homicide—depends largely on the handler's interpretation of the dog's reaction and behaviour.

Was the dog's alert an active alert or a passive alert? Was the alert a response to an outside influence? The behaviour of the dog can be read by only one person: the handler.

"This is why training is a big part of every dog team's work," Jamie said. "Continual training helps us keep our skills sharp, and annual certification ensures the evidence will be upheld in court. We validate to a strict standard. Initial certification for a new dog and handler is done at sixteen weeks. After that, we have to re-certify to the annual standard, which is typically more difficult. Enforcement handlers work together a lot, so I'll validate with the City Police and they'll validate with me. If our evidence is ever scrutinized in court we can show there was an impartial judge validating the dog and handler's abilities."

On the morning I met up with Jamie Jaks was kenneled in another part of the Ministry building. Jamie and I chatted over coffee in his office. The walls were papered with memos and photos of dog teams. A photograph of a man's torn forearm was pinned to the bulletin board—yes, from a dog bite, Jamie confirmed. The victim was another officer, an experienced handler and practiced quarry. The dog that bit him was Keela, Jamie's first German shepherd.

"We start with muzzle training when we teach the dogs to apprehend without protective equipment," he explained. "At a young age, the dogs have poor control as far as release goes. We don't want the dog just to focus on holding onto the protection equipment."

As a rule, during training, handlers wait for the desired behaviour to occur and then reward the dog. Handlers don't "yank and crank"—that's considered "old school." He showed me a short training video of a young shepherd learning to apprehend a quarry. The dog was wagging his tail and barking vigorously while the padded quarry stood motionless against a wall. The trainer ignored the dog. "He's a young dog," said Jamie, "but he knows he has to be down." The dog would not be sent in to apprehend until he was quiet.

"Everything they learn is by reward, but some dogs are just strongly driven—butt-heads, like Keela." He said this fondly. "Sometimes, if they don't do what they've been taught, they need a correction. Jaks is very highly-driven but he really takes a verbal correction from me to heart. He's really a soft dog, not like Keela."

As for the dog bite—nodding to the photograph—serious bites happened rarely during a real apprehension. Keela had done what she was trained to do. The quarry—the officer who was training her—had just misjudged the dog's reach. Handlers are generally good enough at their jobs that nobody needs to get hurt. During a chase or an active search there is a lot of noise, commotion and warning— plenty of time for a suspect to surrender.

If this sounds like police dog work that's because it is; much of the training and work is identical to police dog duty. "There are general purpose dogs and detection dogs," Jamie said. "A general purpose dog can track human scent, apprehend, detect, retrieve evidence—all those things. A straight detection dog is a dog you'll find at the border, in airports, or in a penitentiary. Some police departments have straight detection dogs working for them."

So how does the dog know who or what he's supposed to track? Did they use a scenting article? "No, that's a myth," Jamie chuckled. "We're never lucky enough that the guy leaves his jacket behind for us to use. The dog generally picks up the freshest track available. We might only find a vehicle left in a field, and the guy has taken off running. There are tracks but you can't see them. As soon as the dog hits the track, he's gone, and when he's running, you're gone too! Through the trees, branches hitting you in the face and … well, it's not for everybody."

He laughed and flexed his forearms. He received regular physiotherapy for his arms and his quads for strained muscles from hanging onto the leash, pulled by Jaks. Jaks is a lot of dog—I verified this when Jamie ran him through a few exercises in the training arena. I wasn't familiar with the Malinois, which is smaller than the German shepherd and with shorter hair, often reddish in colour. I once heard the breed described as "squirrels on steroids," and Jaks did remind me of a squirrel in his movements. Everything about him was quick and exact, and he never seemed to move in a straight line. His energy in executing commands was intense.

"They're a high drive dog," Jamie confirmed. "There's a lot of liability, time and money put into these dogs. I can't, for example, just hand Jaks over to a friend for the weekend if I'm going away. If you were to let him out in your backyard—six foot fence? He'd be over it. And if another dog happened to be going by, there might be a fight, and then what would happen? His drive is so high, his work ethic one hundred percent, but if he was a pet I believe he'd be dead by now. He'd have swallowed something whole or run into traffic. He has no fear, and he needs to have his energy put to work. He needs a job."

It was hard to picture Jaks's explosive energy being harnessed for anything as delicate as a scent trail but Jamie assured me Jaks applied his intensity to his work. Sticking to one scent was part of core tracking skills, and the dog had to learn that if his handler started him on one track, he had to stick to that track to get what he wanted—usually a ball or a big play, never a food reward.

"If you have to reward a dog with food he's lower drive. His food will always be number one. Make him feel good about himself, that's the greatest reward. I'm sure it works the same with people."

This gave me hope for Tove. As his confidence slowly improved it seemed he was becoming more interested in cooperating with me. He still had a one-track mind when it came to hunting habits, and was not what I'd call a team-player. He had a pretty good nose for a sighthound but it was impossible to get his attention when he was on the scent of something. What impressed me most about Jaks and the police dogs I'd met was the balance of drive and purpose—a purpose that was connected to the handler.

Some of that was dependent on the breed and some

on continuous training, Jamie believed. As Lorne had pointed out, competing scents can interfere with the main track, so the dog has to learn how to focus and to work with the handler. "Dog tracks, other human tracks, feces, garbage, traffic, cats run through," Jamie said. "They have to totally ignore all that once they've found the track. The dog knows the difference between two people's scent. In a rural setting—grass, fields, bush—not a problem. The trail could be hours old. I did a track once with Keela for twelve kilometers, two and a half hours, and she never quit. Caught the guys by a pay phone."

Not only does each object present its own scent picture but the way the dog reacts to the trail helps to illustrate what has happened. Jamie and Keela once assisted the police in tracking an escaped prisoner. Keela tracked along a grid road, periodically veering into the bush and then back to the road. This happened every mile or so.

"Traffic would come along the road and the prisoner would duck into the bush," he explained. "We followed the trail to a cabin and up a flight of stairs. Keela stood up and sniffed the window sill, and then she sniffed at the door handle. The prisoner had been touching the window and trying different doors. You pick up clues like that from the dog. It's just like a picture."

The scent from an object fans out on air currents. "If you've ever seen a campfire burning, you know how the smoke comes from the fire. Where does it go? The wind takes it. If you can imagine a camp fire two hundred times smaller, to the end of the shell casing, that's where the scent is coming from. Now imagine it on the ground, a little cone of fire, and the smoke carrying it downwind. That's how scent works."

Understanding how the wind works in different situations is key to detecting evidence. For example, as the wind moves down a flat road it planes out crosswise into the ditches. "When the dogs are young and first go out there, they don't know what to do. We cast them around, work them back and forth in a pattern to make it easier to pick up the scent. The dog looks for that scent cone going out, and when he hits the scent cone—there it is! He works his way in and follows it. Soon he learns to face into the wind because that's what brings him the most success. It's natural, instinctive. Now you just work with him in that pattern."

After repeated exercises the dog learns to trust the handler to lead him to the find. In the real world, when the handler doesn't know where the object is hidden, the handler must trust the dog to find the evidence himself. Just as Lorne said, and Jamie now repeated: the handler's biggest mistake was to second-guess the dog's accuracy. A dog handler's worst enemy is doubt.

But trust is a two-way street, as he pointed out, and confidence-building during training is essential. As part of his job, he spent time in school classrooms, teaching kids about environmental protection and law enforcement. The students were always fascinated by the dog, and Jamie explained the role of confidence building like this.

"If you were the slowest guy in a race—the absolute slowest—and I put you on the 50-yard line with some of the fastest guys—big impressive-looking people—and let you win, what would you think? You'd think you were excellent, you're the best, and we'd tell you that. That's what we put into these dogs. We want them to feel they deserve our confidence, and to be sure of what they do— detection work, apprehension, anything—because that's what builds the drive and the attitude they need to do the job for us."

Jamie said that, over the years, he had gained a better understanding of dogs and other animals. He'd learned to pay more attention to detail, to those minute clues that a tracker notices: the way the grass is bent, the direction pointed to by a dislodged stone. He was also more aware of people's behaviour.

"We spend a lot of time travelling around the province, going down every highway, in and out of every little town, going to different investigations. When you're around people, after spending that much time with the dog, you start to pick up on what they're communicating. Not so much from the language and the drama, but the way people act, the way they move. I pick up rapid breathing, slow breathing, apprehensiveness, whether people are feeling insecure, anxious, afraid. I have a good sense of it."

For dogs, communication depends on more than scent and body language. Understanding emotions plays an important role. Reading emotions helps to keep social groups together, and emotions motivate individuals to defend and protect one another. What makes dogs sensitive to human social behaviour is, in his view, bred in the bone.

"From what I see dogs have always been human companions. They've helped us for hundreds of centuries, so they've always been in tune with us. A lot of those special characteristics—the trust and the ability to bond with us—have been selected for. They have the social behaviour that I, as a handler, can understand, and vice versa. I get what they're saying to me, and I understand what other dogs are about. I can pick out which dogs are confident or insecure, and which ones are bullies. Can I do it with people? Absolutely. I can pick out human bullies."

At the entranceway to the Ministry building was a picture of Keela, Jamie's first dog. She was one of half a dozen dogs that have served the Ministry over the past twenty years. It was clear from the stories Jamie shared with me that he still missed his first dog. She had been his work colleague and partner for six and a half years.

"There's a bond there that—unless you've been a police dog handler— most people don't understand. You work together all day, every day, you train together all the time. The dog waits for you every day in her kennel, your steps are coming to let her out. Nobody lets her out but you, and nobody feeds her but you. Everything you do, everything the dog breaths and knows, is the handler."

Jaks was his partner now and Jaks was still a young dog. As a dog team they'd been together for over a year. Every day the bond between them grew stronger, but he admitted that it hadn't started out that way. The working relationship is one that is built over the weeks, months, and years of constant interaction. The strength of that bond is commensurate with time. Jaks and Jamie were still building that relationship.

What Jamie said about relationship-building went far to explain where Tove and I were in our own relationship. Each day we gained a little better understanding of one another. He was starting to be a little easier to recall after a run, and he looked forward to being offered a drink. He liked me to hold the bowl for him beside the car so he could take a few laps. He was sticking close to me when we entered new territory. A creature of strict habit, he often came into the living room late at night if I was watching TV, and stood and stared at me if he thought it was time for me to come to bed.

Usually, I took the hint. Slowly, he was training me.

9 SLED DOGS

-Long may you run-

It's early March in northern Saskatchewan, the tail end of the sledding season. A chorus of huskies greets me as I drive into the yard at Sundogs Excursions, near Anglin Lake. The dogs are a colourful sight against the Jack pine and the snow. Their eyes follow me as I get out of the car—icy eyes, blues and browns, and that all-penetrating gaze. A shiver runs through me. A vestige of wolf fear? Or just the anticipation of a dogsled run.

Minutes later, I'm comfortably seated in a sled while Brad, Sundogs' proprietor, goes through the safety check list. There isn't much Brad hasn't thought of when it comes to managing dog team risks, but then running a successful eco-tourism business in the boreal forest in winter is pretty serious business.

There are about a thousand things that can go wrong in the musher's universe, and most of them have happened to Brad at one time or another—although he strikes as a calm and collected kind of guy. After the safety check, we enter the noisy yard to select the dogs for our run. "I could pick my six best dogs," he deliberates, "but then our run might not be as interesting."

His fur-trimmed hood is pushed back in deference to the mild weather, and his sun and wind-burned face is creased with smile lines. In opting for a more adventurous combination of dogs, he passes to me one of his command leaders, Badger, a handsome male Siberian-Alaskan husky cross. Next he brings out one of his hard working female leaders, the eager Meow-Meow. Meow-Meow is clearly a handful. She can't weigh more than forty-five pounds, but Brad has to dig in his heels to hang on to her.

Badger and I follow Brad and Meow-Meow to the staging area—males on one side, females on the other—and we snap into the picket lines. The rest of the pack howls and barks, and zippers back and forth on their chains in the yard. Brad fetches Kodiak, another calm and collected male, who will run second in the lineup. He'll be paired with Solstice. Lastly, we'll need a couple of power houses in the wheel, Allegro and Arcturus.

Badger and Kodiak stand patiently, the soul of husky courtesy, while I struggle with the dog snaps. I've managed to tangle my mitts in the lines. Next comes the harness; I accidentally put it on backwards, threading Kodiak's feet through the wrong webs. He stands good-naturedly while I twist and re-thread and turn the harness inside out. My fingers feel frozen, even though it's a pleasant minus five degrees Celsius.

By the time I get my two dogs harnessed Brad has staged and harnessed four dogs and clipped their claws. Meow-Meow, frantic to get going, bounces up and down next to placid Badger. She hops the lines and threatens to truss him up, but the senior dog remains unperturbed.

Are we ready? Brad checks the ropes on the sled while I stand on the foot brake, a piece of studded tire that will apply friction to the snow if we need to slow down. Brad then sets the snow hook into the trail base. This is our "parking brake." A second line, the snub rope, is tied to a tree behind the sled. "It's not like a snow mobile, there's no way to turn a dog team off," Brad tells me calmly. With the snow hook removed he moves swiftly to the back of the sled and I hop in up front. The snow hook is secured to the sled frame behind my left ear, and I can feel the whole sled straining forward. We are tethered by just the snub line now. Brad yells above the howling. "Just one thing you have to remember, no matter what: hang on."

Well, two things actually. Keep body parts inside the sled.

Brad pulls the snub line free, and six dogs buck forward. We're off!

The wild characteristics of the wolf seem to run a little closer to the surface of huskies than in other breeds. Twenty years ago, huskies were used in the Canadian North for attending trap lines, moving winter camp supplies, and, only occasionally, for sled racing. Mushers were much more isolated than today, and the dogs might spend their whole lives with just one handler. With more roads to the North, mushers and their dogs aren't quite so isolated, and there are more occasions to travel to racing competitions. Many sled dogs, like Brad's, are socialized well enough to be handled by the likes of me.

As we stood at the perimeter of the dog yard after our glorious run—which had gone smoothly, exhilaratingly smoothly—Brad pointed out, by name and pedigree, each of the thirty dogs in his yard. When he started mushing, almost twenty years ago, he had the good fortune to acquire some very good dogs from racing kennels. They were dogs perhaps not fast enough or strong enough for long competition distances, but well-suited to carrying passengers on short runs. Most of the dogs now in his yard were from his own kennel blood lines. That morning he had been thinking about which dogs to breed for this summer's litter.

Arcturus, an eight-year-old Alaskan husky in his prime, was his best overall command leader and trail leader. Arcturus was a bit more likely to exhibit dominance to other males in the yard, a trait that came with his lineage—his grandfather and his grandmother were also dominant dogs—but Arcturus already had a litter of pups on the ground. His son, Brimpton, would join the team as a working dog next winter. Aster, there, was sister to Arcturus, and the black and white dog was Nelly, "a real sweet dog" that someone had dumped off on the highway a couple of summers ago. Brad had adopted her. "No, we don't need Nelly pups," he said. "She likes to bounce and she's super friendly, but she doesn't have the athleticism of the other dogs, so she never gets enough work."

And so on down the line and throughout the yard. It was quite a family.

Each dog had a low-slung kennel with a neatly painted name sign. The fence around the yard was more to keep visitors from straying inside than to keep dogs from escaping. Each dog was tethered to a private patch of ground by a seven-foot chain, long enough to allow each dog to touch the rear end of the next, but short enough to ensure order. The chain had the added benefit of teaching the dogs to be dexterous about stepping around ropes—important, Brad told me, to avoid tangles in traces.

Most of the dogs in the yard were Alaskan huskies, but, as he put it, the gene pool was deep. Not all his dogs resembled typical huskies. Over the past twenty years, the conformation of the sled dog has changed from the typical burly, stocky dog to one with a lighter build. The new huskies are faster and have better stamina, he claimed. "They don't always have that big wolf face. They're still pretty versatile in terms of going into the bush overnight at forty below. But they're not as raw *utilitarian* as they used to be twenty years ago, when they had longer coats and heavily furred underbellies. Nowadays, you hear people talk about putting belly wraps on their dogs in windy situations on the lakes, so they don't get frostbite on their underparts."

In recent years sled dogs have been racing tremendous distances. The world class Yukon Quest and the Iditarod, to name just two, cover more than 1000 miles in sometimes under nine days. Dog breeding, nutrition, and training strategies have come a long way to meeting these new long-distance challenges. "The new sled dogs are still called Alaskan huskies," he said, "but they're different."

What *hasn't* changed is the high energy and drive of these dogs, and their intense desire to run. "We literally harness that energy and desire, put it in front of the sled, and away they go."

We went up to Brad's cabin on the edge of the woods. I was still buzzing from the run—the steady rhythm of the dogs, the sled runners gliding over the snow—it had been wonderful. Brad made us tea while we talked about sled-racing. This year's Iditarod, the "Last Great Race on Earth," was just over. This is the race said to test the metal of men, women and dogs. International film crews and journalists descend annually at the starting line in Anchorage or in Nome, the finish-line. Brad told me that mushers prepare for at least a year for this race, and each musher has a different race strategy, special diet for the dogs, and his or her own idea about dog stamina and personal ability.

Closer to home were a number of dogsled competitions which Brad had either competed in or was familiar with: the annual Canadian Challenge from Prince Albert to LaRonge, and the two day Torch River Run at Christopher Lake. Mushing is now mostly a recreational activity. Brad is one of a very few professional mushers in Canada. I asked him what had drawn him to this line of work and he told me he'd studied biology and then worked for Parks Canada for a number of years. He loved the boreal forest, and enjoyed teaching people about wildlife conservation. Hundreds of adults and students visited his outfit each winter, taking the short day trips by dogsled or overnighting at the winter camps.

Over the years, he had trained and employed several apprentice dog mushers. No one makes money mushing from races anymore, he told me, although some competitors might make some cash from the race purse, enough to cover a few costs. "If you're a top-notch racer, you might make money selling your puppies," he said. "Mushers come from all sorts of backgrounds and get into it for all kinds of reasons. Sometimes they do it because their families have had sled dogs and it's something great grandpa did. Others do it more as a sport, to really compete. You have some mushers who can barely feed themselves, and others, gentlemen mushers, who have day jobs and can afford to keep a small kennel and do it up right."

The work is physically demanding. Brad, a wiry, compact man in his late forties, struck me as being extremely fit. When I arrived earlier, he had been clearing trail with an axe along the road. Heavy snowstorms at the beginning of the season had bowed the Jack pine over the roads and the trails for miles. "I had to break down and buy a snowmobile to complete the work," he confessed, "but prior to that I made a point of doing all the work by dog team."

Over time, he has learned how *not* to spend his energy, his direct physical energy. "I have fewer issues handling the dogs now than I did in the past. If dogs were still dragging me around like they did fifteen years ago, there'd be nothing left of me."

A musher is like a sports team manager, and the goal is to take that rowdy team energy and direct it down the trail as fast as possible. He said he'd spent the first 10,000 hours, or ten years, just trying figure out how to get down the trail in one piece.

"In the beginning, you are as much a learner as any

dog. You do some reading, you put in some hours, you get some pros to help you out, but you're going to have to make mistakes."

What kind of mistakes? "Dumb mistakes, like taking off with your team and losing a boot—because your boots weren't tied up properly, and you're pedaling," he said. "Or mitts-on-a-dummy-string—because you can't handle a dog on lines with big mitts. All you're trying to do for the first few years is to minimize the injuries. There's a lot of power there, even in little Meow-Meow. When she decides to go, you'd better have your hand on that collar or be ready to lift her from four-wheel to two-wheel drive. You need a strong back, shoulders, and arms, because they want to go."

The first thing a novice musher is likely to do is to lose a team into the bush. "The dogs will take off, go five miles, and hopefully come back without a problem. Or they may bring the sled back in pieces."

Mishaps can be more serious, as in, "Now that dog is tangled up, and if you don't get her untangled she's going to injure her shoulder, or the other dog will think he's being bitten, and try to take a bite out of his neighbour. And then you've got a fight on your hands."

Dog fights are rare, like accidental breeding, but are a fact of life for mushers. He has learned to appreciate dog compatibility. "Versatility in dogs is real nice when you're running a lot of animals, because otherwise it's like having too many extraordinary children; you have to manage too many things. You're trying to get the dogs down the trail as efficiently as possible, and if one dog can only run with *this* dog, or has to run on *this* side and can only run in *that* position—well, that's a lot for you to remember."

A musher soon learns who should and shouldn't be on a team together. Fighting isn't commonplace; in truth, he was surprised that there were so few fights. "One of the nice things about running Alaskan huskies is that they usually get along really well. Being reared in a pack, they understand how a pack is to be run, and that includes how the musher is expected to behave."

As long as he avoided particularly bossy dogs, he could generally count on being able to pick out a few dogs from another musher's yard, put them into his own yard, and an hour later, run them together behind a sled. That was the *ideal* situation, but it happened more often than not. At a mass race start there might be twenty or thirty teams of four, six, or eight dogs each, lined up and waiting for the race to begin. Parked beside one another, they'd be excited and barking, but they wouldn't be trying to get at each other.

A telling thing occurred, however, if one pet dog on a leash happened to pass between the line of sled dogs. "All of a sudden, every dog will be growling and snarling! Because that pet dog is not sending out the right kind of message, the one that says, 'I'm part of this pack.' Other dogs just have no street cred' with sled dogs."

The competence to run a team comes with time and experience. Competence might imply a kind of minimum requirement for the job, but *in*competence in this environment is doomed to end badly. "As you come along as a musher," he said, "you want to feel competent enough to do what you need to do to get that team safely down the trail. But there's something called 'Instant Musher Syndrome,' which mimics competence. That's when everything is just fine for the first two or three runs, or the first year, or maybe even just the first hour you're out there. The dogs are behaving perfectly, the trail is fine, and there are no equipment failures. You start to feel, 'What's the big deal?' The next thing you know the dogs come around a corner, you hit a rut, and you're thrown fifteen feet on your arse against a spruce stump. And the dogs are gone."

Instant Musher Syndrome: over-confidence. There is a difference between over-confidence and the competence that comes from knowing how to actually run a dog team.

He admitted that a person can only think so far ahead, before things change up and a completely new situation is at hand. In the dog musher's world, dealing with the unknown on the trail is not unlike dealing with the unknown in life. As Brad put it, "Here's you, here's the dog, and then there's a universe of possibility for the next ten seconds. What's going to happen?"

It could be that dog number two in the team is tangled and dog number one is tangled, but nobody is yanking yet so you must decide whether to go to the dog at the back—before he's under the pressure of six dogs and could really be hurt—or should you check the snow hook? "And that damned snow hook had better be in the snowpack," Brad declared. Or should you let the snow hook pop, and move the whole team twelve or fifteen feet forward to that tree up ahead? *And then* attend to the tangled dogs? "You don't know all this until you've actually done it. It *is* kind of thrilling to be alert enough, aware enough, to manage all that." Brad grinned broadly. "I don't think I'd be doing this if there wasn't variety. The dogs provide variety."

One of the most important lessons he had learned from the dogs was the value of inner composure. "If I lose it," he explained, "if I lose my focus, my composure on the inside, that's going to be manifested on the outside. And then everything will break down—from the way I handle the dogs, to what they're reading from me. If I'm having a bad day, they have to give more energy to straighten me out before things can smooth out up front."

It might look like controlled chaos, with all the bouncing and barking going on, but he'd be moving quickly and decisively to get things done. "I'll be saying, 'Okay, that dog is the next one that needs my attention, so I'm going to do this, then *that's* what I'm going to do *next.*' And sometimes, if I'm really tuned in, I'll ask myself, 'Okay, what am I *not* doing right that is putting the dogs off?'"

Inside the cabin, we sat by a window looking out on the forest, with our feet up on the heat register and our mugs steaming before us. There was simplicity in the way things were arranged inside the cabin. Beyond the window lay tangled white wilderness.

The paradox struck me: the unpredictability of life versus infinite possibility. The adventure we seek versus the order and sequence we need to accomplish things.

"The tension between the known and the unknown is like the yin and the yang," Brad said. "We're always drifting between those two points in our lives, in our relationships with people as well as with dogs."

We each wondered aloud whether or not we were comfortable dealing with the unknown. "I don't know what's *good*," Brad mused, "what coping mechanisms I have or don't have. I'm not a psychologist. I know that the dogs help to bring those coping mechanisms to my attention. When I'm out there, am I having a bad day or am I having a good day? How does that affect my dog? Maybe there isn't anything special going on in the dog's head, but it's still valuable for me to think of him as my mirror. The dog doesn't know he's the mirror, he's just reflecting what he sees. The mirror doesn't reflect anything but what's there. You interpret it."

I asked Brad how the lead dog manages to command the other dogs. "Lead dogs are always in the lead," he answered. "It's more of a literal thing, because you can have not-very-dominant dogs that can be good leaders. Even quite submissive dogs can lead. All of a sudden something switches on when they're in lead, and they're a completely different animal. Kodiak, for example, is super quiet, but when he gets out on the line, he's ready to call the shots. He's not a great command leader, but he's a pretty good trail leader. The other dogs don't have to listen to him—they just follow the leader in line."

There are two types of leaders: trail leaders—that just try to get down the trail as fast as they can—and command leaders—that take you exactly where you want to go. "Badger learned, early on, to be a good command leader. In the past ten years, he's trained about half the dogs in this yard. You put a young dog—one you hope has the desire and inclination to be a leader and to learn the commands—with an older dog like Badger, and they just learn."

The mush commands are *gee,* turn right, *haw,* left, and *whoa* to stop. *Hike* has the same meaning as *mush*: let's go! With a good team, one that has trained together for distance racing, the commands are more subtle. Brad couldn't say whether the dogs understand they are working as a team all the time, but their cohesiveness improves the more they work together.

"That's one thing about training for distance racing. You see something completely different emerge in your dogs. Your relationship with them also changes. What they did today they could do with their eyes shut. Yes, they're working as a team in that they're going in one direction, and they have the speed and the power to get up hills with passenger weight. But they're rarely on the trail long enough to get into the "zone" that distance dogs get into. When they're in the *zone* they become totally focused, with a real "we're-serious-about-this" kind of attitude."

He described this shift akin to becoming "an in-earnest hunting wolf pack." "You'll still see some of that bouncing at the start-lines of races, but trained distance teams tend to be flattened out by the middle of the season. They're more serious and more disciplined. They're still having fun, but they're waiting to get into that zone. And it's a really beautiful thing to see. *That's* what I call a dog team."

In the zone, the dog's gait starts to match and there is a rhythm to the run, a rhythm between you and the dogs, as he described it. Your body language becomes very subtle, and your commands become subtle too. Now you're running with the same leaders every day, and everything seems to fall into place.

The more you run with the same dogs, the more *intention* the group shares. There is a kind of anticipation of the next move, a telepathy between team members. Brad remembered once stepping off a sled and being about to give a command to a couple of dogs. They had paused on the trail to choose a direction.

"I don't know how much or how little I moved—maybe it was just my eyes. I was looking straight into the dogs' eyes because they had turned when we stopped. I made one little eye movement, and they went exactly where I wanted them to go. It was very, very subtle. To me, that's what you're going for when you're developing a relationship with your team. Everything becomes more subtle and under control. Even though it sounds like the opposite, that kind of communication is far more effective than yelling, '*Gee, gee, gee!*'"

To an outsider mushing appears to be a harsh and solitary lifestyle. The pack has each other, but the musher's life seems very isolated. Brad admitted that the responsibility for so many dogs did claim a big chunk of his life. That being said, most mushers had spells of exchanging chores so they could take time off.

"Because the dogs have their home out there, they're not like a pet dog that has to be let out in the morning and at four o'clock. You have more responsibility but at the same time you have a little bit more flexibility and independence than with a pet. You still have to clean up after thirty dogs every day," he laughed.

When asked if any of the dogs were companions, he said, "They *can* be companions, but they're not needy companions. Brimpton, like the other puppies, will come into the cabin to visit. Once in a while he still sits on the chesterfield with me. He chews on that plush dog and we'll hang out."

Brad once made the mistake of taking a dog named Mike for a walk in the woods on the leash by himself. Mike didn't want anything to do with the walk, and was anxious to get back to the yard and rejoin the other dogs. Brad realized the dog had never in his life been outside the company of five or six dogs. Why would he want to go that far away on his own? "He just hated it. I never took Mike for a walk by himself again."

In a few short weeks spring would arrive in the North, and with spring and summer came "down time" for Brad and the dogs. Like the off-season athletes they were, they'd need the time to recuperate from micro-injuries and to rest for next season. Summertime was too warm to train, but the dogs would get out, two or three at a time, and run down the trail with him, or follow him on his bike. The dogs' coats became lighter in summer. If he did any dry-land training with a cart, it would be just a mile out and back on a cool day, with lots of water. "When people aren't around, dogs do a lot of sleeping," he said. "They just crash. We cut back on their feed so they don't get overweight. Training begins at the end of October."

As the days were beginning to lengthen, Brad had been walking with Brimpton and a couple of other dogs in the late afternoon. "It's nice to have their company to do that, but I wouldn't say they're good at recall. The more time you spend with them from puppyhood, the better recall will be, but if they get a squirrel or a snowshoe hare in their noses—or in their heads – I might not see them for half an hour. They won't go far, they'll never get lost, but they won't be at my side, heeling. No way."

What I had enjoyed most about the dogsled run was the perfect silence of the forest. Not a single motor vehicle disturbed the peace. The only sounds were the dogs panting and the sled runners on the snow. The speed was exhilarating, the rhythm of the dogs steady, mesmerizing. It was hard to leave Sundogs.

Brad called out something as he waved from the cabin porch. What was that?

"Long may you run!" he shouted again.

He'd said it on the phone, the first time I called him. What did it mean?

"It's from a Neil Young song. It means just what it says. May you have a long run."

I thought about it on the drive back to Saskatoon. Long may you run. The longer the run, the better you get to know me; the better you get to know me, the smoother the ride. The smoother the ride, the more enjoyable the run. The implications were boundless.

I suspected Tove and Badger, had they ever met, would have little to say to one another. Both were pack animals, both half-wildlings, both nine-tenths instinct— but they would never share the same intention. Perhaps if Badger was suddenly stranded in an urban setting, he would lose some of his princely bearing. Being part of a pack is no small part of a dog's confidence—his assurance of his place in the world.

The better you get to know me the smoother the ride. When I got home, I emailed Brad with my interpretation. He wrote back: "I also just like it as a parting blessing, or the benediction it implies for life. Long may you run."

10 SEARCH AND RESCUE DOGS

-Who else teaches us humility?-

On October 10, at 9:30 a.m., the K-9 Conservation Officer with the Ministry of Environment received a call from the Prince Albert RCMP detachment. Daryl and his dog, Zoro, were at work on the eastern side of the province, finishing up night patrols for illegal hunters. The dispatcher reported that an elderly man with Alzheimer's was missing from a care home outside Prince Albert. The search had been underway for more than twenty-four hours. The missing man was last seen walking toward the city, wearing slippers and a light wind-breaker.

RCMP officers and volunteers from the community were combing the area between the care home and the city. A search aircraft was surveying the banks of the North Saskatchewan River. So far, the plane's heat-seeking device had found no trace of the man. Daryl, who was familiar with the area, suspected the tree canopy would impede the plane's heat detector. It was just the kind of area where a search dog should be deployed.

Search and rescue missions aren't normally part of the Ministry of Environment's mandate. Missing persons are a police matter, but when asked for assistance, Daryl did not hesitate to respond. He put the dog into the truck and headed west to Prince Albert.

By midafternoon, he reached the search headquarters. After going over the map with the search manager, he drove out to meet the search team. A footprint had been found on the river bank. He selected an area that had not yet been searched, and put the dog to work on a ten-foot lead.

Daryl guided Zoro ahead of him. They followed a virtual grid, checking each quadrant of ground as they walked. They soon reached a slump in the riverbank, a drop-off where the man could not have passed. They doubled back and searched in the opposite direction. Daryl began to doubt the veracity of the footprint.

He returned to search headquarters to consult with the search manager. Dinner had just arrived for the search team. As hungry as he was, he knew they had to make the most of the remaining daylight. He checked the plane's search pattern again, and returned to the river bank. This time, he turned Zoro off leash so the dog could work more efficiently.

As they searched Daryl was mindful of the direction of the wind. Mentally, he roughed out the flood plain in the same grid pattern. Zoro zigzagged diligently back and forth. The sky grew dark and the air became perceptibly cooler. Daryl knew the chances of finding the man alive were dwindling. For several nights, the overnight temperature had been below zero.

It was becoming difficult to see his footing in the dim light and he was just reaching for his flashlight when he saw Zoro halt and give the alert. He looked in the dog's direction and saw a man—slumped down between two fallen trees. As the dog approached, the man's arm gestured weakly. He was alive.

Zoro stopped and waited for Daryl to climb over the tree stumps to reach the man. The man was wedged between two trunks, as if he had slipped backwards from sitting on a log. Trapped between the fallen trunks, he was too weak to free himself. Carefully, speaking calmly to the man, Daryl extricated him and checked him over for injuries.

The man was exhausted and unable to speak. His face was ashen and he trembled violently. He was in his shirtsleeves and stocking feet—no sign of a jacket or footwear. Daryl took off his uniform jacket to warm the man, and radioed the search headquarters to report their location. They would need a four-wheeler to bring him out of the bush and an ambulance to meet them on the road.

From the corner of his eye, he saw Zoro, still poking around in the bush. It was past seven p.m., three hours since they'd arrived at the search headquarters and nine hours since they'd left the eastern side of the province. Zoro was thirty feet away from them, wagging his tail and looking expectantly at Daryl. Daryl went over to see what the dog had found. There, in the grass at the dog's feet, was the man's wallet.

Zoro was the only dog in these chapters I did not have the pleasure to meet. By the time I caught up with Daryl, Zoro had been deceased for half a dozen years. I had heard part of this story from Jamie in Prince Albert. Zoro and Daryl's successful rescue had become part of the legendry of the Ministry. When I tried to find more details of the story in the local newspaper archives, I came up empty-handed. An online search for Zoro and Daryl's names returned only a brief mention in a Canadian Search and Rescue magazine.

When I found Daryl's contact information at the Ministry of Environment in La Ronge, I couldn't believe my luck. Luckier still, he responded at once to my inquiry. Search and rescue dogs aren't common in Saskatchewan. The southern third of the province is hard to get lost in, and the rest is heavy bush, crisscrossed with rivers and lake systems. Thousands of miles of muskeg discourage hiking in the North, and even canoeists don't venture inland without an experienced guide.

"The terrain makes it physically difficult to do search and rescue," Daryl said. "For most of the searches, we're required to work in and around or through water. The dogs do well detecting things in water, yes, but it's a lot of water, and a lot of area to cover."

Typically, the RCMP search for missing persons in back country. During the years that Daryl worked with Zoro (and his first dog, Scout), the RCMP conducted about a dozen back-country searches each year. Daryl was called in two or three times a year to assist.

The search dogs used by the RCMP are trained to a national standard, and the RCMP are fairly choosy about using their own search dogs. That being said, the enforcement handler world is a small one, and Daryl trained regularly with other police dog handlers. The RCMP were familiar with Daryl's dogs and their skill level.

Daryl's personal interest in rescue operations began some time before he became a dog handler for the Ministry. He recalled being stationed as a conservation officer in Greenwater Lake Provincial Park when the RCMP came looking for a search helicopter. A child had gone missing from a pow-wow on a nearby reserve. The Ministry normally contracted helicopters during the summer time to conduct poaching patrols. "We freed up a helicopter to come down for the search," said Daryl, "and I went along with their officers."

The pilot and the RCMP search manager were up in the front of the helicopter, and another RCMP officer and Daryl took the back seats, where visibility wasn't as good. It was late in the fall. The little girl had been missing overnight. The helicopter searched the area around the pow-wow site, and followed visual transects from a creek that served as a boundary line.

"We flew for close to an hour," Daryl said, "and I thought we had pretty much dusted the area in terms of what we could do. And then I looked down—I remember it distinctly—and saw her, the little girl. She was huddled at the base of a tree on the edge of a creek."

The helicopter pilot and the officers couldn't believe that a three-year-old had survived a night in the bush on her own. The helicopter landed and the team got the child into the helicopter. The RCMP officer was the one who returned the girl to her family, but Daryl remembered getting out of the helicopter in the midst of the crowd, "so our uniform was there." It was a proud moment for Daryl.

It was a pivotal moment in what would turn out to be Daryl's future search and rescue career. The second such moment came in 1994, when he was training to be a dog handler with the Ontario Provincial Police in southern Ontario. This time, as a search unfolded near Tisdale, Saskatchewan, Daryl could only watch from a distance. "It was a very large search for a young girl named Ashley Christianson, and a pretty sad story. She became lost one day when she was playing with her friends. At this time, my dog, Scout, had been doing really well in the training course, but we still had another month to go before we could start working in the field. I remember watching the search on the national news, and thinking that I wanted to be there—I wanted to put my dog to work and to give it our best shot. But I just had to watch it unfold on TV because we weren't ready."

The search for Ashley Christianson ended tragically with the recovery of her body, but that search also led to the formation of the Prince Albert North Search and Rescue group, made up of community members from around the Spruce Home area. The community wanted to be better prepared to assist future missing person searches. After Scout and Daryl finished their routine detection training for Ministry duties, they joined the rescue group for more search training. Daryl eventually became a search manager.

"It was all part of the outdoors, which is what my job

as a conservation officer is all about. It's what I love. That, and being a canine handler. It was the best of all worlds for me."

Most of the dog team work for the Ministry was straight forward detection work. In the early days of the unit, however, just proving the canine's value to the Ministry was a challenge.

"Scout first proved herself when she was six months old by finding some evidence left by night-hunters, and it helped to get a conviction. That really helped to establish the canine program for the Ministry. But there were some tough calls to be made, because it was usually only after the field officers had exhausted all other efforts that they'd think to bring the canine in—long after the fact. Usually they'd be calling for me and Scout and a miracle. Luckily, Scout was such a good dog she pulled off a lot of miracles."

One of Scout's miracles took place in the southeast of the province, after a moose that was seen hanging around some local granaries suddenly disappeared. The investigating conservation officers discovered a burrow pit, an excavation hole used for road in-fill, not far from the granaries. Fresh dirt had been pushed back into the hole. The field officers asked Daryl if he thought his dog would be able to assist. Daryl travelled south from Prince Albert and put Scout to work.

The landowner consented to have the land searched. Daryl and Scout began in a grid pattern across the burrow pit. Scout scratched and dug in one corner, and that was all Daryl needed to suspect that something was there. The Ministry's most valued game resources at the time were white-tailed deer, moose and walleye fish. Handlers trained their dogs to detect illegal game caches by burying or hiding small pieces of hide or meat for the dogs. Scout's training, and her own particular work ethic, were about to pay off.

"We got a shovel and took turns digging," Daryl said.

"We got close to four feet down, and were thinking, 'This is a lot of dirt to move with a shovel.' We checked the dog again, and she jumped down into the bottom of that hole and kept digging. We decided we'd better get a backhoe in there."

It was now getting late in the evening. The landowner suddenly recanted his permission to search. The field unit then had to get a search warrant to resume digging with the backhoe. As Daryl described it, with each stroke of the scoop, he watched and waited and worried: that moose had better be there.

Suddenly there was a thud, and the next thing Daryl saw was a moose leg, sticking straight up.

"That carcass was buried over seven feet deep in the earth," he said, "and Scout pinpointed it exactly." Later, a bullet extracted from the moose was matched forensically to a firearm belonging to the landowner.

I asked how the dog knew what to look for. "During training," he said, "different collars are used in combination with specific commands. We have a detection collar and use the command 'Seek,' for those game-scents the dogs are trained to detect."

Most canine agencies use a variety of collars. "The Ontario Provincial Police used a detection collar, an obedience and agility collar (just a regular choke-chain collar) and a tracking harness. We also had an aggression collar, which was a very heavy leather collar—very new and stiff. It was a kind of ritual for them when you put the collar on. The more you work with those commands and those collars, the more the dogs learn to associate them with particular activities."

Search and rescue is a canine specialty, but the way in which the dog works is the same as for general detection duty, he explained. Searching for people is done either by trail tracking or by air scenting. "You're either going to locate a track and then track to that individual, or you're going to be searching air currents, hopefully downwind from the scent cone they're giving off. Quite often the method you use will depend on how quickly you're called in after the search gets underway."

With air scenting, the dog searches for fresh human scent, as Lorne and Jamie had described earlier. Daryl used a search collar and the command "Lost" to locate missing persons. There was no point starting to search at the immediate site because it was already contaminated with the searchers' scent. It was more important to find out what efforts had been made, and then to choose an area that had not yet been searched.

"Depending on the weather and wind conditions, the dog can usually find fresh human scent. The further the scent cone drifts from the person, the more it dissipates. The dog will work the area, and if they pick up human scent, that's what grabs their interest."

As the handler guides the dog in the search, he assigns each area a "find probability." In order to make an educated estimate, the searcher assigns a probability to the area—what are the odds of finding someone in terms of a percentage? "It's never one hundred percent," said Daryl. "Some people might say so, but in the search and rescue world you know that's not a possibility."

Too often the outcome of missing person searches is the recovery of human remains. The bush and muskeg are unforgiving territory. "Lost individuals don't fare well after a few days in the bush," he said. "Logical thinking—what would I do in this situation?—doesn't work in most search scenarios. People panic, they take off clothing when they're hypothermic, they wander in bizarre directions."

Search and rescue, like other police dog duty, is demanding work, both physically and mentally. It is hard on dogs and handlers alike, a young man's occupation, Daryl observed. He'd retired from the canine unit, but his job with the Ministry continued. He remembered the dogs he had worked with, and his handler days, as the highlight of his career as a conservation officer.

Scout, he remembered, was a very methodical tracker. The police dog handlers he trained with said that Scout liked to show off, because she wouldn't just cross the pavement when she was tracking, she had to track exactly where the quarry had *stepped*. Zoro was a good-natured dog with enormous personality. Zoro had been intended for the Prince Albert Police Service, and had come to Canada from Yugoslavia with his brother, who went to the Calgary Police Dog Service.

Zoro was a bit of a clown. Daryl recounted their first somewhat inauspicious meeting. "Zoro had just taken a dump inside the police station, and I took him outside while the police handler cleaned up," he told me with amusement. A sense of kinship must have kindled between them, because when the Prince Albert Police decided to replace Zoro, Daryl jumped at the opportunity to bring him on with the Ministry.

Zoro and Daryl worked together for seven years, and Zoro retired happily to Daryl's home at the end of his days. For his role in the rescue of the Prince Albert man, Daryl was awarded the RCMP Commanding Officer's Commendation, the first individual outside the RCMP to be awarded this distinction in Saskatchewan.

When asked what the dogs had taught him personally, Daryl replied, "Patience. The value of patience." Then he added, "And not to take things too seriously."

This surprised me, but his meaning became clear when he told me about another of Zoro's fine moments.

A few days after the rescue of the Prince Albert man, Daryl met the search manager at the search site for a debrief. The search manager wanted to know the exact location on the riverbank where the man had been found. Said Daryl, "So we went down the trail, Zoro was with me, and we stood exactly where we'd found the man. We were looking up at the tree canopy, trying to figure out—for the sake of future searches—why the plane had missed him.

As we were doing this I saw Zoro give an alert. There he was, wagging his tail, like, *Come and look.* So I went over, and sure enough, there was something in the grass. There, were the man's dentures."

Coincidentally, the first thing the lost man asked, when he was recovering in the hospital was, "Where are my teeth? Where is my wallet?"

Zoro had found all three—man, wallet, and teeth, in three separate finds.

The point for Daryl was that, as much as Zoro was valued for his rescue skills, he was, after all, a dog—and one that brought laughter and humility to the job. "They do remarkable work for the reward of a ball or a game," Daryl said.

There had to be a great life lesson in that.

11 THERAPY DOGS

-Trust and unconditional acceptance-

It was the second day of final exams on the university campus, but inside Convocation Hall the mood was anything but studious. No typical meet-and-greet therapy dog session, this; it was more like a fun fair. There were popcorn and cookies, grab bags and lint-rollers (for removing dog hair), and bulletin boards featuring study and de-stressing tips. Five dogs, the star attractions of "PAWS Your Stress," stood ready and waiting to receive attendees, vested in the red St. John Ambulance therapy dog jackets.

A circle of chairs ringed each dog, and the students were lined up around them. I joined the queue to visit a chocolate Lab named Dakota, who had travelled three hours from Regina with her handler to be here. Dakota usually worked on the palliative care unit at Regina General Hospital, but she read this young crowd like a pro. She folded herself at the feet of a freshman art major, and the two of them passed a few minutes in warm wordless exchange.

Dakota was trying not to be distracted by Rita, a little

blond dog of Spaniel descent, that had her own circle of clients a few feet away. Rita's visitors were taking pictures of her on their phones—presumably to send to classmates still locked away in the study halls. Rita had props, including a bird-sounding toy that sorely tried a Lab's natural instincts. Rita struck me as a bit too lively for this line of work, but her handler assured me she was a regular visitor at a school for severely handicapped children, a job that required a second level of testing.

And here was Kisbey, the energetic boxer owned by my work colleague, Colleen. Kisbey had a penchant for attempting to lick faces, which she freely demonstrated at every chance. Kisbey was—is—irresistible, and, once she has you in the beam of her joy, you can't help but feel cheerful. The first thing people do when they meet Kisbey is smile, and then they begin to laugh. Some people wipe tears from their eyes—a sure sign of de-stressing.

It isn't just the calming effect of the dogs at work here. An emotional exchange seems to occur: *I'm so glad to see you! Me too!* A tail-wag of recognition, a warm hand, a calming stroke, a salty lick of appreciation. As people reached out to touch Kisbey—one handed, two handed—they couldn't get enough of her. A middle-aged woman sat on the floor and encouraged Kisbey to lick every square inch of her face, while she giggled with childlike abandonment. My colleague, Colleen, the Research Chair of One Health and Wellness at the university, and one of the co-organizers of the PAWS Your Stress event, beamed in Kisbey's lime light.

The PAWS Your Stress event was a collaboration between the Department of Sociology, Student Health Services, the School of Public Health, St. John Ambulance Therapy Dog Program, the Office of the University President, the Western College of Veterinary Medicine and the School of Massage Therapy. At the moment, the massage tables stood empty. The massage therapy students had been upstaged by the dogs.

***

A surprising array of institutions have added dogs to their arsenal of mental health aids. Not only has it become more common to see dogs in seniors care homes and hospitals, they are showing up in more unlikely places, such as addictions counseling centers, prisons, public libraries and after-school reading programs. Where I live, St John Ambulance is one organization that tests and qualifies dogs for therapy visiting. The goal of the St. John Therapy Dog program is to provide love and support to people through interactions with dogs.

No specific training is required, other than a test of the dog's obedience and general unflappability. The dog has to be "bomb-proof," as Colleen told me—meaning completely tolerant of loud noises and lots of hands-on contact. Most importantly, the dog should enjoy contact with strangers.

I dropped by Colleen's house one Saturday morning to chat with her about her three therapy dogs. When I arrived, Kisbey and two other therapy dogs, Anna-Belle and Subie, were barking and scuffling behind a baby-gate in the hallway. The barrier was meant to spare me their eager attentions. I had expected therapy dogs to be… well, more relaxed. But as Colleen pointed out—and as I'd seen for myself—sometimes canine exuberance is just what the doctor ordered.

The idea that dogs make us feel good isn't new. I asked Colleen about the research evidence. Research shows that pet ownership reduces human heart rates and blood pressure, and that dog owners have a greater chance of surviving heart attacks than non-dog owners. Patients with dogs have shorter hospital stays, and adapt from illness and injury more quickly than their dog-less counterparts. One of the most obvious benefits of having a dog is that they exercises us.

It seems obvious, too, that dogs counteract social

isolation and perhaps even depression, but when it comes to hard proof of the mental health benefits of dogs, the evidence is harder to measure. No one denies that dogs give us a sense of well-being, but how do you measure happiness, support and a sense of security?

These are some of questions that mental health researchers try to tackle. Colleen said it hasn't always been easy to be a social scientist measuring the impacts of pet therapy. Her research has been awarded funding from the Canadian Institutes of Health Research and other academic sources. She has worked with seniors, youth and prison inmates on a variety of mental health and wellness projects. In spite of the scholarly papers she writes and the interviews she gives on human healing with animals, some people still think what she does is a little "fluffy."

"But that's okay," she said to me. "People used to think the world was flat too."

Colleen's dogs are qualified by St. John Ambulance as therapy dogs. She brought them into the living room, one at a time, to introduce them. First, Anna-Belle, an Old English English bulldog cross, the lead of the therapy trio. Anna-Belle had a face full of wrinkles and an adorable snuffle—easy to see why she was the poster-child of therapy dogs. Colleen and Anna-Belle regularly visited seniors' homes. "The first time we visited," Colleen said, "there were about twelve people sitting in a circle. She went to the first person for a minute, then the next person, then the next. She was very methodical. There was one chair left open for a person who came late, so she went back to see him." Colleen laughed. "She has better social skills than some people I know."

Next, came Subie. The brindled boxer greeted me enthusiastically. His wayward tooth made him look like a cartoon boxer. "A happy clown," Colleen described him, "but not very assertive, so he gets the low pressure assignments." She and Subie regularly visited an addictions treatment center.

When Kisbey was released into the living room, she fairly *flew* into my lap—all forty-five pounds of her. Kisbey, Colleen confirmed, was the dynamo of the three dogs. Kisbey and she had a new project, visiting a psychiatric prison.

This year was Colleen's sabbatical leave from the university and she had been delving deeply into the therapy dog scene. Her website documented her travels and described the dogs' adventures in pet therapy. She and Anna-Belle had just returned from a two week course at a dog psychology academy in Illinois, where Colleen had been learning to train dogs. "We were learning how the dog *thinks*, basically," she clarified.

She'd also been learning about other programs that use dogs for mental health aids, like the "Puppies for Parole" program at Missouri State Prison, that teaches inmates how to train and care for dogs as they prepare to integrate with society, and the Walter Reid National Military Medical Centre, that trains dogs for war veterans with post-traumatic stress disorder (PTSD).

Only that weekend in North Battleford a war veteran with a PTSD dog had been refused service in a local restaurant. The management didn't believe the man had a disability. When the soldier refused to disclose the nature of his disability, he and the dog were shown the door. Colleen explained how the dogs help to regulate emotional triggers in PTSD survivors, and are trained to wake their owners from nightmares. Veterans with PTSD often withdraw socially after returning from active duty, so the dogs offer much-needed companionship and interaction.

Colleen is not a therapist herself but as a researcher she is interested in how dog therapy works. Enrolling in the Illinois dog-training program was one step towards better understanding dog communication. At the Centre, owners of dogs with behaviour problems surrender them for two weeks to be retrained by learner-trainers. Colleen and other trainers-in-training learned on the job how to work with these dogs. "Some were bratty, some were quite vicious," she said. "While we rehabilitated these dogs, we were learning what we needed to know as trainers."

At the beginning of the course the instructor asked the participants, on behalf of their canine charges, "Will you still love me when you get to know me?" Colleen thought this was an interesting question. "We don't always *get* that in our society—that dogs have needs that we have to understand and accommodate. We have to learn to respect the needs of dogs, and to communicate with them as dogs."

She has learned to work more effectively with dogs by interpreting the world through their eyes. What she looks for now in a training scenario, or a therapy dog session, is what the dog is communicating *to her*. Being aware of what is being communicated allows her to facilitate interactions between the dog and the participant. It is particularly important to be able to recognize a dog's discomfort, restlessness or inattention. The dog must feel well-connected to the handler to feel secure enough to respond to unfamiliar people in a sometimes unfamiliar setting.

On the one hand, interacting with people comes naturally to the dog; on the other, these interactions can be intense. By the end of a session, the dog is typically exhausted. Colleen compared it to keeping up an hour-long conversation with a stranger—draining.

The bond between dog and handler is one of trust and two-way communication. A textbook illustration of this trust was exemplified in a case of a child receiving play therapy in the presence of a therapy dog. When the therapist handler validated the child's feelings, the child reacted unexpectedly by straddling the dog and putting a tight hold around its neck. The therapist expected the dog to resist, or even to snap, but instead the dog didn't move. The dog looked to the therapist for reassurance, and somehow sensed what was needed in the situation.

Colleen believes that what takes place between the dog and the participant is a form of emotional communication. When I asked her what that communication might be, say, in the first thirty seconds of "love-in" with Kisbey, Colleen said she didn't know, but she'd often asked herself the same question.

She and Kisbey had recently been visiting a psychiatric prison—these were called animal-assisted activities, rather than therapy. Such interactions are less goal-oriented than therapy but can still be therapeutic, she explained. When she first proposed the project, the prison administration was slow to respond. After six months of navigating through the official channels, she was given permission to work with the prisoners, but there was still some resistance from the prison staff.

"On our first visit we arrived early and there seemed to be a lot of confusion. The guards didn't think we should be there—the women shouldn't be petting dogs, they were in there for committing crimes—that kind of attitude. They thought it wasn't secure for me and it wasn't secure for the dog to be with these women. I was pretty nervous the first time."

Each female inmate selected for the program was to spend twenty minutes individually with Colleen, Kisbey, and a prison representative. Colleen carefully considered which dog was best suited for the job, and selected Kisbey for her high positive energy. On their first visit, after close to an hour of waiting, the doorbell rang in the visiting room to signal that one of the participants had arrived. The door opened, the inmate appeared, and when she saw Kisbey for the first time, she lit up like a Christmas tree.

"It was a moment of pure joy," Colleen recalled. "She hadn't seen a dog for something like a decade. Imagine loving dogs and not petting one for that long? And it was perfect, because she loved boxers. She had pictures of boxers on the walls of her cell."

The inmate had indeed been looking forward to

Kisbey's visit, and the two of them, as Colleen described, were just "*there*, in the moment." Kisbey lavished her with attention for about five minutes, and then the inmate asked Colleen if she thought that dogs knew whether people were "good." Kisbey choose that moment to roll on her back for a belly rub. "And Kisbey doesn't usually do that," Colleen said. "I said to the woman, 'She just met you five minutes ago and she already trusts you unconditionally.'"

There was no doubt in Colleen's mind that Kisbey was responding at that moment to the woman's extreme need for affection. Dogs excel at being in the moment. On a later visit, after a violent event at the prison, Kisbey wanted nothing to do with this same inmate. I asked Colleen if she thought Kisbey's belly display was a sign of trust or one of submission. Like so much communication, interpreting behaviour has everything to do with the context. Did Kisbey sense what was needed at that moment or did Colleen's interpretation of Kisbey's behaviour provide the validation the woman needed?

Most therapy relies on the therapist's understanding of the client but, as Colleen pointed out, "We don't really understand what is happening between the dog and the person. It's beyond understanding. Maybe that's why people sometimes use the word *magical* to describe it. I think there are some things that science is unable to explain."

She has noticed that trust develops quickly when an animal is brought into the therapy setting. "If I'm a counsellor and you're my client, and you like the dog, you're going to transfer some of that trust to me," she said. "A few studies in addictions have shown this. You'll start to trust me quicker because you like the dog. The trust with the dog seems to be almost instantaneous."

The therapist needs the trust of the client for therapy to be effective. One of the challenges of treating mental illness is establishing trust with the client. Emotional trauma often damages interpersonal trust, and can impair the ability to form healthy and trusting relationships. Once the world has been shown to be an unsafe place, trust takes time to reestablish. This holds true for dogs as well as for humans.

Emotional stability and emotional resilience are nurtured by self-confidence and a sense of security. A child's self-esteem, for example, grows with her mastery of the environment. Similarly, a dog with confidence knows its place in the world. Key to developing and maintaining self-esteem is the idea of validation—that we have personal value and that our feelings are valid. As Colleen pointed out, dogs affirm and validate us every day.

Take, for example, how happy dogs are to see us. Every day we are treated to their wholehearted joy, even when we've been away for only a few hours. Part genetically-programmed wolf-puppy? Part can-opener fever? Part stick-itch? Perhaps, but largely their enthusiasm is a testimony of love. And it feels good to see them race to the door to greet us. Who else shows such undiluted eagerness for our company.

Could validation be one of the active ingredients in pet therapy? "Dogs allow you to be present in the moment, without judgment," Colleen said. "People are just allowed to *be*. How often do we really get to be *just me*, without judgment or expectation?"

If there is one common truth she has observed, time and again, in every therapy setting, it is this: human happiness comes from love and acceptance.

Colleen's interest in dog therapy evolved from her work in equine therapy. She saw many amazing things happen around horses. "With horses, you also get to be just *you*. At the same time, the horse looks for a leader. If you have confidence and purpose, the horse will follow you anywhere. The horse knows a leader. It trusts a leader. It's not so different with dogs. And having their confidence is hugely satisfying."

Consistency in handling and training gives a dog a sense of security. In pet therapy or animal-assisted activity, the dog isn't looking just for leadership, but he appreciates the attention and the affirmation. In Illinois, after retraining the dogs surrendered by their owners, the trainers trained the owners. "They have pretty good success," she said of the program. "The owners have an hour and a half session when they return to reclaim their dogs. Then they have some homework to do, and they receive ten one-hour sessions to learn how to maintain the behaviour. For those owners who do not follow up—yes, the dog goes right back to the same behaviour. You can almost tell who will succeed after that first session, because some owners are asking, 'Am I doing this right?' and the others are saying, 'Oh, my little baby.' But it's not just about the love. It's also about establishing boundaries."

Dogs are sensitive to interpersonal dynamics, and being sensitive to the dog's signals can give the therapist or handler an important clue or segue into a conversation. Follow the dog's lead, other handlers advised Colleen. It wasn't unusual for individuals to show a completely different side of themselves during these brief encounters. A staff member at the addictions treatment center said that she often discovered new things about a patient during pet therapy sessions. "I recall one staff member in particular who said she'd never seen her client so happy and at ease as she was with the dog. It gave her a great sense of satisfaction to see her client so happy."

Colleen often started her own visits by asking, "Have you had a dog?" She found it a great ice-breaker. Most people have fond memories of dogs and respond positively to visiting dogs. At the prison, she noticed how swiftly attitudes changed among the staff after her first visit with Kisbey. "The dog was loving it," she remembered, "the participants were loving the dog. And the guards were worried about my security?" She believed the guards saw these women—some of their highest needs inmates—in a somewhat different light after they had a chance to observe some of these encounters.

The therapy process might not be *just* about the love but, in her view, the benefits of dog therapy are *mostly* about the love. Dogs have the power to improve the quality of life by encouraging connection, fostering acceptance and providing a daily dose of laughter. We might not be able to measure the power of kindness, reassurance and encouragement, but we're pretty certain of what we feel.

I couldn't say with certainty that Tove had bonded with us by now but I do remember, with a slight hitch to my heart, the first time he greeted me with pure gladness. He wagged his tail and danced around, wriggling with excitement. I stroked him and praised him, and leaned against him as he leaned into me. It was a milestone in his emotional development, and in our relationship.

12 ASSISTANCE DOGS

-Patience, character and devotion-

Odie is a retired helper dog, a cheerful twelve-year-old black Lab with bright eyes, white eyebrows and a grizzled chin. She lives with Naomi and her family but formerly worked for Alicia, Naomi's sister-in-law. Odie's whole family joined me to talk about Odie at Alicia's home one afternoon.

Though officially retired, Odie was in the habit of regularly visiting Alicia as part of the family. It was clear to me that Odie and Alicia still shared a very special bond. After opening the door for Alicia's wheelchair and following her inside, Odie planted herself behind Alicia's chair and inspected me solemnly.

Assistance dogs are the super-heroes of the dog world in my books, so I was a little bit in awe meeting Alicia and Odie. Besides the amazing tasks they perform, assistance dogs are companion dogs *par excellence*. One look at the guide dog literature told me that an important predictor of dog and handler success was personality compatibility, so my first question to Alicia was: how did she and Odie come to be matched?

Alicia was fifteen when she first applied for an assistance dog. The application process was lengthy and every aspect of her daily life was considered: her type of disability, her medications, family members, work and home environment. After the first interview with the sponsor organization she was required to take a personality test. A year passed while she was on the waiting list, and finally the letter came inviting Alicia and her mother to northern Ontario for the selection process and training.

When she arrived at the training center Alicia discovered there were seven dogs for eleven applicants. Clearly, some of them wouldn't make the cut. Added to this pressure was the fact that the dogs weren't "finished" in terms of working experience. All the dogs were between eighteen months and two years of age. The dogs rotated between the candidates over a three week period so that everyone got a chance to work with every dog.

"Odie was very nervous. She didn't know me," Alicia said with understanding. She described what it was like to work with a different dog each day. The dogs also took turns staying with the candidates in their rooms at night. After working with all the dogs, Alicia said that Odie "just felt right."

Assistance dogs are the eyes, ears, hands and feet of their handlers; seeing-eye dogs for the blind, hearing dogs for the hearing impaired, seizure response dogs for people with epilepsy, alert dogs for diabetics. There are dogs trained to provide comfort and companionship to autistic people, and dogs to assist patients with dementia. The greatest benefit these dogs provide is to enable their people to enjoy more active and independent lives.

Odie was trained to help mobility-impaired individuals. Retrieving objects, opening doors and drawers, turning lights on and off, and guiding in crowds requires a high degree of cooperativeness and a low level of excitability. The two most common breeds selected for guide and assistance dog work are the Labrador and the Golden retriever. The hallmarks of these two breeds are a willingness to work, a calm disposition and a high level of initiative. In the United Kingdom, the most favored guide dogs are Labrador-Golden retriever crosses, believed to combine the intelligence of the Lab with the exceptional "desire-to-please" of the Golden. Breeds other than Labs and Goldens are sometimes chosen, and guide dogs may even be selected from animal shelters, but often guide dogs come from specially bred lines of service dogs, as did Odie.

The dog's character relies heavily on up-bringing and experience but genetics plays a role too. Some trainers go as far as to say that certain physical traits predict a dog's suitability for guiding—specifically, right-pawed dogs (leading from the right paw). Paw dominance relates to left and right brain hemisphere processing of stimuli. Testing pups for guiding aptitudes starts as early as seven weeks, when the dog's inborn tendency and temperament begins to show. Lots of testing and lots of observation helps to single out the exceptional dogs. If the pup makes the grade she will spend a year with a foster family to become properly socialized and learn obedience basics. Staying more than a year means risking she will bond too firmly to the foster family. After the pup is returned to the professional trainer, the *real* training begins.

Some sponsor programs match dogs to candidates *before* training begins, and others train the dog and candidate simultaneously. Dogs may be preselected for certain candidates using canine personality tests. During the candidate-matching process, training staff watch to see how the dog will respond to the candidate and the candidate to the dog. Height, weight and stride have some bearing on the appropriate match, but what pairing really comes down to is a feeling of compatibility.

Some guide dog trainers claim they have little to do

with selecting the match, because the dogs tend to select their people. So what is it that makes a dog and prospective handler feel comfortable together? Some trainers say it's more akin to chemistry between people than anything else.

When I asked her why she thought Labs were so well-suited for this work, Alicia said, "They're smart and they're loveable." As to what was special about Odie, "Her heart," Alicia answered. "Odie would do anything for me."

It hadn't, however, started out that way. Once the match was made, an excited Alicia brought an excited Odie home to Prince Albert. Odie was very nervous for the first few days in her new home, and Alicia remembered her being sick in her room. "I'd be scared too," Alicia said. "Odie is just like me. She doesn't like being the center of attention."

Kris, Alicia's brother, described what it was like for the rest of the family. "For the first six months nobody but Alicia was allowed to play with the dog, and whenever Odie had her harness on, nobody but Alicia was allowed to talk to her. We had to adapt. For certain things we had other people helping out, but other than that it was 'hands off' for six months. When the harness was off Odie could play—when you took her out to the bathroom. It was important for Odie to make that bond with *only* Alicia."

The bond between assistance dogs and their people often depends on what happens in those first few days together. Odie's training wasn't finished—and would never be truly finished. Like all service dogs, she would have to continually practice her tasks in order to keep up her skills. Her performance improved as her bond with Alicia strengthened.

It was challenging for Alicia's three brothers to ignore Odie—who was, after all, a loveable dog. The family decided to get a second dog, but the distinction between the "working dog" and the "family dog" was hard on Odie. "The other dog got all the attention," Kris said.

"Eventually we had to give that dog to another family because it wasn't fair for Odie."

Odie was very much a "people" dog, and, like all dogs, she needed a variety of work and play to keep her content. She clearly possessed the compassion and character to do what she was trained to do. As she gained competence and confidence, she learned the names of new objects and was able to retrieve them.

Odie's most challenging work assignment was going to school with Alicia for Grade 11 and 12. She had a hard time concentrating in the classroom, and Alicia's classmates didn't help the situation. They didn't always know or follow the rules. "They'd be petting her—and she loves to be petted, what dog doesn't?" said Kris. "And they'd feed her," Alicia added ruefully.

But Odie's loyalty to Alicia never failed in the years that she served her. "It could be minus forty outside, and if I dropped something she'd go back out and try to get it," Alicia said. When Alicia was ill with influenza Odie refused to move from her bedside for days. "She lay right next to the bed. If I needed anything, or even made a sound, Odie would automatically bark or get up to go get my mom."

I sensed that Odie, for all her heart, had a very strong personality. Personality builds on temperament, but what else is in the mix? Some guide dog trainers believe that compatible personalities are not only key to the successful placement of assistance dogs, but to the placement of *all* dogs. This is what helps to make a strong owner-dog bond.

Kris and Naomi, and even Alicia herself, commented several times during our conversation about how alike Odie and Alicia were in terms of personality. When I asked Alicia what Odie had taught her about herself, Alicia answered frankly, "She's shown me how passive aggressive I am."

That elicited a big laugh.

Kris explained. "When you're in the position where

you need someone to do something for you, you use as many techniques as you can. Odie can't just go make herself a sandwich. So one of the things Ode does if she hasn't had a walk, for example, and she thinks she should have, is passive aggression. She doesn't bark and she doesn't complain. She just won't eat. She refuses to eat. She'll make you feel guilty. Now *that's* passive aggressive."

Strong character is expected in an assistance dog, because character tempers determination, and determination is what is needed to complete difficult tasks. Odie wasn't a perfect angel—and what determined character is? She sometimes exercised her prerogative by "talking back" to Alicia–especially if she was being scolded for something. "She likes to follow me back to my room, barking at me," Alicia said, grinning. Naomi agreed that Odie sometimes talked back to her. "She just seems to have something to tell you."

As mentioned earlier, one of the characteristics that helps to explain the strength of the bond between dogs and humans is emotional intelligence. Emotional intelligence has been carefully selected for in assistance dogs in particular. It takes a special kind of character and a high degree of awareness to put another's welfare ahead of your own. To be empathetic requires recognizing a state of mind different from your own. Recognizing other people's intentions and emotions supposedly defines human intelligence—as distinct from animal intelligence. Yet another definition of human intelligence that fails to apply only to our species.

Odie was Alicia's constant companion for three years. "I never had many friends when I was growing up," she said. "Odie became my best friend. She was always there. I could talk to her about anything, and it actually seemed she could understand."

After Alicia graduated from high school the opportunity arose to move to an assisted living apartment in Saskatoon. The assisted-living accommodation, however, did not have the resources to keep assistant dogs. Up till then, Alicia's family had performed all the tasks for Odie's daily upkeep.

Like any young person seeking independence, Alicia faced a tough choice: to continue to live at home with her parents and Odie, or to move to an independent living arrangement. "I was devastated," Alicia said, remembering having to make this decision. A few years later, her supported housing arrangement *did* get the resources to accommodate assistance dogs, but by then Odie had clearly and irreversibly retired from work.

"I'm glad she is living with Kris and Naomi now," Alicia said. "She'd be a beginner helper dog if she came back to it now."

"It's not that she doesn't know how to do things," explained Kris, "but when she has had the freedom not to work, she doesn't *want* to do it."

"Work coat on, work coat off," Naomi added. "She knows she doesn't have to work."

Odie's assistance dog background was still very evident, particularly when it came to understanding a broad vocabulary. Naomi, who spent the most time with Odie now, said she sometimes tested Odie's vocabulary. "I'll ask her to fetch something random—like an empty peanut butter container—and she'll often go do it."

Odie has always been sensitive about relationships, and was usually good at judging peoples' intentions—except for one time, as Kris recalled. Back in their courting days, he and Naomi used to practice ballroom dancing at home—an activity that Odie strongly disapproved of.

"We had to put Odie in the other room when we were practicing, otherwise she'd go crazy barking. She just didn't like it. Maybe she thought we were wrestling."

While we'd been talking, Kris and Naomi's two-year-old son, Holden, played quietly in the corner of the room. Odie showed little interest in what the child was up to. "She's not really one for kids," said Naomi. "I'm not sure if it's because they train it out of them—not to go to children—but she doesn't seem to want to be around little boy antics. She's very cautious around Holden."

Alicia told us about a recent Thanksgiving gathering, when, on the first evening at the family home, Odie placed herself outside Holden's door for the night. According to Alicia Odie still knew who needed watching in the family. She had resumed her caretaking role without any direction.

This story surprised Naomi and Kris, who hadn't noticed Odie's behaviour at the time. As they remarked on this Odie suddenly got up from beside Alicia's wheelchair and gave me an enthusiastic lick. She knew we were talking about her.

Several times during our conversation Odie gave me well-measured licks and wagged her tail, getting her whole body into the gesture. She seemed to be demonstrating she was part of the family and had something to contribute to the conversation. Naomi now observed that the difference between Odie and other dogs, even other Labs, was that Odie seemed more human. "I know it's likely me anthropomorphizing," she said, "but her expression, her attitude even, seems more human."

In answer to my question about what they had learned from Odie, Kris said, "I'm sure Odie has changed us. I certainly appreciate animals' personalities more. I find it very interesting to watch her interact with people." Naomi said, "Dogs are pretty good examples of unconditional love. They're also mirrors for our emotion. Odie is easily hurt by harsh words, and they don't have to be directed at her. She picks up on everything. Arguments in the house really disturb her."

When I asked Alicia more generally what Odie had taught her she answered that Odie had taught her patience. "Odie was quite 'hyper' at the beginning, so to work with her I had to be patient. And Odie had to be patient with *me* because I don't have the clearest voice. I am amazed at Odie's level of understanding."

Meeting Odie made me wonder what combination of genes and environment produced such things as work ethic, endurance, concentration and compassion—in deference to behaviours like hunting and herding. Clearly, some dogs are better at the caring profession than others. Perhaps every dog owner wonders if their dog has what it takes to be an assistance dog.

I found myself measuring Tove for helper-dog potential that very evening. As I examined his paws, he rolled onto his back and stuck his legs straight up in the air: his dead-hound-in-the-middle-of-the-road look. Ears splayed flat, jowls stretched in a floppy grin, he shut his eyes and refused to look at me. As it turned out, he is left-pawed– not assistance dog material—but clearly he has other qualities.

As Tove's phobias were dropping away, one by one, his true personality was emerging. He was remarkably gentle and soothing to be around—it even crossed my mind that he might make a good therapy dog. Perhaps these were the behavioural trade-offs for not being overly protective. He was accepting, unobtrusive, and easy to be around. He was still a bit wary of people, and not very good at picking up on emotional cues—but, day by day, he seemed to be a little more optimistic about life.

13 DOG RESCUE

-Be the leader your dog thinks you are-

Tove and I occasionally met up with the other members of his pack at the dog park. Grendel was one of the forty dogs seized by the SPCA. A handsome-looking male, with a broad streak of Scottish deer hound, Grendel weighed ninety pounds and stood close to three feet at the shoulder. An overcoat of coarse grey hair covered his dark undercoat, from the mane on his neck to the tip of his tail. He was an arresting sight beside his mistress, Fina, with her shock of red hair and tattooed arms and legs.

When the pack was divided, and Tove shuttled off to Alberta, Grendel had remained at the Saskatoon shelter. The dogs from the pack differed in appearance and condition. Beyond the general sighthound characteristics—shyness, quiet manners and a keenness for rough running play—they seemed to have little in common. Some had never been indoors, some were in uncertain health, and a few had wasted muscle and hook worm infection. A few dogs were friendly with people, and others were very withdrawn. The best explanation for such an assortment of hounds was that they were intended for coyote hunting.

Fina had started our local sighthound club a few months after adopting Grendel so that the pack could remain in contact and tear up the turf together. Club members got together to exercise the dogs and to compare notes—helpful in those early days after adoption. The hounds we saw regularly seemed to have adapted quickly to their new lives. When I met up with Fina we talked about how the dogs were doing, what behavioural challenges we were struggling with, and the general peccadillos of the sighthound personality. Months might pass between getting together, but we picked up the thread of conversation easily.

I wish I could say Tove's rehabilitation resulted from the counsel of my dog-wise friends, but in truth his adjustment—and my education—evolved more slowly. Time is a great healer, and gradually Tove was achieving "normalcy." He still preferred to be left alone in the bedroom to following me around the house, an independence that was typical of his breed. For short spells he would grace us with his presence, parking himself at one end of the couch. He continued to be a piano buff, with distinct musical preferences. Friends remarked on his progress, and it did seem his attitude towards humankind had shifted.

Along with his new-found confidence the joys of dogdom opened up to him: a ball, a squeaky toy, a wriggle on the grass. And treats—especially dried wild meat. The breakthrough with treats meant he was motivated enough to try obedience training at home. With the enthusiasm of the new convert he learned to *sit, lie down, shake a paw*, and—magically—*stop*. I couldn't find "stop" in the training manual, but there it was.

The command, *come*, however, continued to elude him.

We had discarded the bell for a whistle and, if I was lucky enough to blow it when he wasn't on the trail of something interesting, he more or less recalled. More or less. In addition to these developments I had ceased to be so obsessed with his past. I no longer wondered if his preference for wild meat was from being fed road kill (those perfect teeth) or whether he was someone's cherished stolen pet. He was happy and that was enough for me. When he was happy I was happy.

On a summer evening, about eighteen months after their respective adoptions, Fina brought Grendel over to visit Tove. Grendel, with his small fine head and shaggy body, was named after the ugly troll from Beowulf, Fina told me. "Ironic," she admitted, "because he's a bit of a coward."

Grendel was younger than Tove and very unassuming in his pack manners, but his size was imposing, and Tove gave him his space accordingly. The two dogs didn't meet and greet like other dogs—whether they shared some rough history or felt brotherly competition, it was hard to say, but they did not play together the way we hoped.

I asked Fina how she came to single out the remarkable-looking Grendel from the other dogs at the shelter. She told me she'd been seeing him in her head for years. There were supposed to be two dogs in her life— Grendel was one of them, and she was still searching for his companion. "I've always known what they would look like," she said. "I pictured these two dogs, one on either side of me, one dark, one light. Big dogs. I could see the dark one had a small head but I couldn't tell if it was a greyhound—and greyhound wasn't quite right. The other dog is female and blonde, and she has a beard. I thought the female was coming first, but then I found Grendel."

When she first saw Grendel at the shelter she wasn't ready to adopt a dog. She had gone there with a friend, thinking her friend needed a dog. The moment she saw him, cowering at the back of his cage—"thirty pounds underweight, greasy, and totally autistic,"—she *knew* this was her dog.

***

The idea of rescue is a powerful notion: to be saved, singled out, not because one deserves to be chosen, not for some personal quality, but by sheer pointless luck. In the scheme of things, we all need rescuing at some point in our lives.

People have been rescuing dogs, and vice versa, for a millennium; every stray that ever became someone's "forever" dog is, after all, rescued from some obscure condition. And yet in the last twenty years or so dog rescue has evolved almost as a movement. Dog rescue is big in North America, and ranges from private family-run operations to loose networks of individuals and privately funded agencies. Some rescue organizations are breed-specific—greyhound rescue, pit bull rescue, French bulldog rescue, to name a few. Does altruism alone prompt rescuers to rehome and rehabilitate these dogs?

A number of dog writers have written wonderful accounts of dog rescue at home and abroad. Steven Kotler, who has written entertainingly about dog rescue and the meaning of life in northern Mexico, noted that the human response to helplessness is innate. "Sympathy leads to empathy, and empathy is always the point of no return."

We know what's in it for the dogs, but what's in it for us?

"I was living in an apartment where I wasn't allowed to have a dog," said Fina. "I had a week to find a new place—they wouldn't let me take him without a landlord's consent…well, fair enough." She wasn't too worried that anyone else would be interested in the thin black dog while she home-hunted. "He didn't like people and he didn't like other dogs," Fina said. "He was not interested in food. He didn't even show fear. His soul had totally shut down."

She decided that if he was supposed to be in her life, if she'd been seeing him in her head for years, it would happen. "Not that I was totally fatalistic about it," she said. "You have to have faith first, and then try your hardest to make it work."

By the time she found a place to rent that would accept dogs four other people *did* see what she'd seen in Grendel. Luckily, the SPCA had held him for her. Did she ever doubt that she could rehabilitate him? She admitted she *did* wonder. "But then I thought, maybe he is supposed to teach *me* something."

Before she could see what was under that rough coat, she had to build him up. He had lost a lot of muscle, probably from being tied up all the time. In the early days, she could only walk him for about half an hour. "He was so weak that he could only hold his leg up to pee for about five seconds. He was afraid of other dogs, and covered with scars. He'd probably been in fights and been unable to get away."

He was not afraid of people but he wasn't interested in them either. At home, he slept continually, common with sighthounds, but his disengagement was extreme. Gradually, by walking him and feeding him carefully, he regained his thirty lost pounds.

But Grendel had issues beyond low weight and low engagement. Once he had bonded to Fina, he began to show signs of separation anxiety. He would collect things from around the house when she wasn't there, and then he began urinating indoors. "He felt quite ashamed about it," she said. "He'd be excited to see me, and then he'd see that I saw his puddle, and he'd act ashamed." She went so far as to set up a video camera to investigate what was happening. He was fine throughout the day, but about an hour before she came home he would begin to pace and whine and finally to howl. Then he lost control of his bladder.

"I realized it was an emotional thing," she said. "It wasn't exactly separation anxiety, because he wasn't getting anxious until later in the day. It wasn't that he couldn't hold it until I got home either. I live near a school, and the kids come home shortly before I do, so I think they were tipping him off."

The trouble was that she couldn't always come home from work at the same time every day. Another potential issue was her boyfriend—that classic disturber of dog-and-mistress relationships. Many dog writers have commented about the anxiety a dog feels when he is displaced by a new relationship. As social animals, too, dogs prefer to deal in certainties. Social rules about things like hierarchy, routine and pattern, reassures pack members. Grendel was becoming anxious about his one and only pack-member, Fina.

She decided to hire a trainer to address Grendel's anxiety problem. The trainer recommended a few psychological shifts, one of which was to introduce the idea of earning affection. "That bothered me," Fina admitted. "I did that for a while, but it was too hard on *me*, to dole out affection for good behaviour, and ignore him the rest of the time." She understood the theory—that too much praise coming at unpredictable times confuses the dog and he doesn't know what he's done right—but turning affection on and off just felt wrong to her.

Another of the trainer's suggestions was to improve Grendel's confidence by giving him little tasks to do. "He enjoys doing things for us—going back and forth between my boyfriend and me, lying down and obeying me. Sometimes he carries a couple of cans in his doggy backpack. Maybe he feels useful," she said.

One recommendation that she did endeavor to follow was to introduce more structure to their lives. Most new dog owners quickly learn that dogs really do thrive on routine. Fina hadn't grown up with a lot of structure herself, so this was a personal challenge for her.

Raised on a farm, she had a lot of personal freedom growing up, and with that independence came the expectation of self-sufficiency. From an early age she was expected to get up, make her lunch and get herself to the school bus. "The dogs I grew up with were farm dogs, and in my family my dad was the alpha," Fina said, laughing. She described herself as very much an "omega"—neither dominant, nor submissive. "I have zero interest in human hierarchy," she said. She was, however, the first to admit that being independent wasn't the same as feeling secure.

She adopted a cat to keep Grendel company during the day, and, with a few more interventions, Grendel improved. The problem with adopting a medley of solutions is the difficulty in knowing what worked in the end. Interestingly, over the same period of adjustment, Fina found she, too, was changing.

In her job as a geochemist she managed a laboratory with a small staff, and she'd never enjoyed her management role. Before Grendel arrived she didn't socialize much outside of work. She didn't like to ask people to do things and was more comfortable with independence. Slowly, however, she was learning to be part of a team.

She said she thought Grendel might teach her something, and when I asked her what that was, she replied without hesitation: confidence.

"At first I thought Grendel just needed to know what was expected of him, but, over time, I realized that he really *does* need structure. All the time. He doesn't do well thinking for himself. He really needs an alpha. It's good for him to have me in charge. I used to believe that just loving him would make him feel better, but he's really taught me how to be strong for someone else."

Learning what it means to be a good alpha has shown her that she has what it takes to be a leader. This has affected her whole outlook, and she has started to accept being part of a human pack.

"He's taught me how to socialize. He's a bit of a conversation piece, to begin with. People want to talk to us," she laughed.

Big life changes don't occur overnight, of course, and

Grendel still has trouble understanding people. As with Tove, Grendel continues to struggle to comprehend how to play with other dogs. "He's better with other sighthounds, but he still can't figure out the game," she said. This is why she thought he still needed an alpha dog as a companion. The idea of a second rescue is never far away.

I've often wondered how much our past experience influences what we're willing to take on. Sometimes, blissful ignorance is all we need to try something new. Not knowing what you're getting into with a rescue dog is a gamble, but it's one that a high proportion of dog owners bet on successfully.

On the half dozen or more occasions when Fina and I have discussed our rescue dogs, we never once spoke of altruistic motives. Perhaps that's because it never occurred to us that we'd done anything but gain from the rescue experience. Far from satisfying any selfless motives, dog rescue has taught us something more valuable: a successful rescue, one that removes all traces of ill treatment and neglect, and allows the dog to shine with good health, is ample reward in itself.

Some dog people say the dog gravitates to the neediest person in the family and forms the strongest bond with that person. This is a variation on the theme of the dog choosing *you*. If, on a cosmic level, we all eventually need rescuing, then in some respects dog rescue does lend itself to the meaning of life.

Not every dog story turns out as rosy as Grendel and Tove's tale. The last chapters are not only about what dogs teach us but speak to difficult issues in the dog world—the hard-to-train dog, animal shelters, end of life, and what our vets can tell about us from our dogs.

14 REACTIVE DOGS

-The learning experience is the thinking experience-

The dogs are brought into the training arena one at a time. Since there's no such thing as a bad dog let's call them what they are: reactive dogs. These are the tough cases, these are the scary ones. For some of them, the next six weeks may be their last chance before the animal shelter.

Fortunately this arena is also where last-ditch-effort meets realistic hope of remedy. It is Thursday night at Lois's practice arena, the first evening of Reactive Dog Training. Lois doesn't call what she does "obedience training;" instead, she calls it "creating a better behaved canine citizen." I can only picture one dog, Max, as a citizen of some primitive Celtic society. Max is an English sheepdog-wolfhound cross, and over a hundred pounds of trouble.

It's hard to imagine a more challenging combination of genes than the persistence of the herding dog and the killing efficiency of the large hunter. It takes both of Max's owners, a husband and wife team, to get Max safely into the arena and behind a barrier. Next, comes Sweetie, a female husky-collie cross. Sweetie appears to have some coyote in her. She was taken too young from her litter, and then abandoned. She barks and lunges incessantly, and her handler struggles to keep track of her lead, her head halter and a bag of treats. Following Sweetie, Bad-boy Jake slinks into arena, and then a border collie named Pix, who tows his owner behind him. Last to enter the arena is a second husband and wife team with a little guy, George—a growler. George's master leans against the wall with his arms folded and glares at the little dog, while his mistress stares at her shoes.

The dogs are all assembled now, each with a corner of the arena or long piece of wall to themselves. They know what to do next—which is fortunate because no one can hear Lois's instructions over Sweetie's barking. Tonight is step one: the dog's name and then a treat, the dog's name and then a treat. Food is a "hind brain" communication, and a signal that something good will follow.

I first heard about Lois from my colleague, Jill. Originally, I had wondered if Tove and I might benefit from her help. About a week before I visited Lois, however, Tove had turned a corner in his training; he'd actually halted when I called him from a field he wanted to explore. Comparing him to these dogs here certainly put our own challenges in perspective.

Lois is well known in the agility world. People tend to find their way to her through word-of-mouth. She is a soft-spoken, petite woman with smile-lines at the corners of her eyes. She doesn't call herself a trainer, although she has offered courses in agility for many years. With reactive dog training, she is more interested in improving individual dogs' lives than in producing a well-trained dog.

But, to back up a minute—what exactly is a *reactive* dog?

"A reactive dog is a dog that reacts negatively to his or her environment," Lois answered. "Lots of dogs have behavioural issues because they weren't properly socialized, or because people did not know how to train them. I started reactive training because I sometimes come across these out-of-control dogs at agility classes. They can't continue in agility because they just can't think."

The goal of reactive training is to make life easier for poorly-controlled dogs and their people. Lois' own objective is to keep these dogs from ending up in animal shelters—because that is where poorly controlled animals end up.

A dog that reacts to a perceived threat cannot *see* or *hear* us, she explained. In the words of Brenda Aloff, one of the founders of the reactive training approach, a dog in "hind brain mode" cannot learn. The hind brain steers automatic responses including the fight or flight state. When a dog reacts adrenalin is released, and certain kinds of neurological activity become blocked. In order to *take in* the handler's commands the dog must use the front brain, or the cognitive part, what we call the "thinking" brain.

"Reactive dogs can become adrenalin junkies," Lois said, noting that adrenalin stays in the system for some time. "The reactive state—the state where the dog can't learn even the most basic commands—sometimes becomes the norm. We know the learning experience is very much the *thinking* experience, so we have to help the dog to *get* there."

Reactive training techniques are designed to make reactive dogs less volatile, but they work for non-reactive dogs too. Food treats are used to shift the focus from the stressful situation to the handler. The "name and treat" exercise is later paired with the "connect with me" exercise. The idea is to condition the dog to look to the handler—first for the reward, and later for reassurance.

With repetition, looking to the handler becomes automatic. "At the most basic level, the dog is being taught to rely on the handler to interpret the situation," she said. The handler's job is to reassure the dog. That reassurance calms the dog in situations that might otherwise make him react negatively.

"Start by removing distractions," said Lois. "Start in the bathroom where it's quiet, if necessary. It is important to understand that a dog's learning is situational, which means that every time the environment changes the dog has to re-learn the task. Most dogs don't generalize between performing a task in one environment and performing it in another environment—in the kitchen versus outside, for instance. Big difference."

This helped to explain why Tove seemed to follow commands inconsistently. "Come" in the kitchen did *not* equal "come" in the dog-park. Repeating the commands in different environments, she assured me, would gradually reinforce them. Calmness was key. "Everything is done calmly. Calm is needed in order for the dog to process the command."

Obedience, in her view, is not really about behaviour at all. "Obedience is just teaching the dog to sit and stay and come and lie down. What we're trying to do with reactive training is put these dogs into a more comfortable state of mind. Lots of times the owner's inconsistency has caused the reactivity and the stress. In the dog's mind somebody has to take charge. I don't like using the word 'dominant,' I think that's an old-school way of thinking, but if you look at it like a family, the mom and dad are in charge, right? And the kids have to follow their rules. I think it's the same with dogs. They need somebody to be in charge—or they will feel obligated to take on that role, even if they are really insecure dogs."

As Fina had discovered, and Colleen had deconstructed, leadership encourages and supports dogs. This is especially important for insecure dogs. So, I concluded, you're really training the people, rather than the dogs? "Absolutely," Lois answered without hesitation. "It takes some people longer than others to realize that in order to fix a broken dog, *you* have to make some changes in *your* life."

It takes a fair bit of commitment to do this, she went on to say, but unfortunately many people just want a magic pill. "We are used to instant gratification, and it's not just first-time dog owners who are guilty of this." By first-time owners she meant those who might not have known what they were getting into with a rescue dog ("and due credit to them," she added, "for getting help"). Even experienced handlers sometimes struggle with that one "odd-ball" dog.

What causes reactive behaviour? On the whole, she believed, reactions are instinctual behaviours. "Reactivity may be part of the dog's genetic wiring," she said, "or buried deep in negative experience. Reactions don't always make sense to us, and behaviour that is natural in one breed may be unnatural in another. Terriers, for example, were bred to bark so they can be heard underground when they're digging out rodents. A Labrador, removed from her litter mates too early, may bark incessantly at any stressful situation."

Dog communication is one of the biggest challenges for first-time dog owners (and some second and third-timers). It seems like an obvious place to start—to ask what a behaviour means—but surprisingly few new dog owners start here.

"People often don't understand what they're seeing. You need to watch the dog's body language, the way they watch *our* body language—how they move their ears, how they move their whiskers. They're telling us stuff constantly."

One of her pet peeves is images of children hugging dogs. "People think it's cute, but you wouldn't if you knew anything about dog language. You see dogs leaning away and doing what we call "whale eyes," where you see the whites of their eyes. Their ears are pinned back, their tails are tucked under their butts, and they show a lot of lip-licking, trying to calm themselves."

The second most common reason people fail to understand their dog comes down to human variability.

On the whole, human behaviour *is* inconsistent, she observed, which is hard on animals that are hard-wired to survive by reading signs and signals.

Sometimes behaviour problems are the result of unrealistic notions about the time it takes to train a dog. "People sometimes think they will get a dog and the dog will just *be* there. They don't realize you have to train them to be well-behaved, that they don't just turn out that way."

Also, she underscored, all dogs really *do* need a lot of exercise—all of them—to be mentally fit. The time invested in training and socializing dogs—just hanging out with them—is a huge part of turning out a well-behaved dog.

I was coming to realize that Tove's gradual improvement had more to do with spending time with him than direct efforts to rehabilitate him. What Lois had told me agreed with what other dog-handlers said about the importance of bonding. "You have to have a strong bond for cooperation," she emphasized, "and you get that bond by working with them, and learning how to communicate."

Socialization means practicing the social skills necessary to meet the world at large, and handling challenges with social grace. "Socialization is not just about playing nicely in the dog park," she said. "They need the skills and habits that are necessary to participate in society."

Dog parks were another of her pet-peeves because she believed a lot of reactive dogs acquired their fears from dogs in dog parks. It's not just the mix of dog personalities one encounters there that presents challenges, but the variability in attitude about what is acceptable or unacceptable behaviour.

One of the techniques in reactive training used to shift the dog's attention from the potentially threatening situation to the handler is to train the dog to accept more eye contact. This is the "connect-with-me" exercise. "Eye contact with the handler helps to improve impulse control," Lois said. "Impulse control is something lots of reactive dogs don't have. We need their attention to communicate with them and reassure them—*before* they get stressed out over something. We're not coddling them, we're being respectful, showing them there's nothing to fear, and that we'll take care of them."

Eye contact can mean dominance and send a potentially aggressive signal to dogs so we have to be mindful, she pointed out, not to use a challenging stare. In getting eye contact from the dog, an approximation will do. Eventually eye contact will transition to seeking permission from the handler.

"We have a piece of food in our hand and we bring it down to the dog. If he snaps at it or reacts unacceptably, we just take it away. It's done very calmly, not a lot of chatter going on. Ideally, once we have sustained eye contact, we start teaching impulse control. Eventually, we want them to ask our permission for that piece of food." Asking permission is just a step away from asking if something is safe.

Lois is also fond of "clicker training." Clicker training, she believes, is the fastest way to get a desired behaviour. "The clicker isn't just to get the dog's attention. It's like a camera that takes a picture of the behaviour you want—click—and then pairing it with a reward. When they're doing something you want, and you click, they know they're going to get a reward. At first you have to click and treat repeatedly, so the dog associates the sound with the reward. If you've clicked when they're doing the *wrong* behaviour you've effectively told them what they're doing is *correct*. People's timing and consistency is the most challenging part." Lois paused and murmured, "The humans are always the most challenging part."

Could she tell the difference between an abused dog and a neglected dog? Lois thought she could. "With neglect, you get a dog that just shuts down and doesn't feel or react—because they are social animals. With abuse you get more reactivity. I don't think there is a difference in the way you handle a dog that has been abused versus one that's been neglected. In reactive dogs training, I do pretty much the same thing for all of them. "

She has come across relatively few dogs with serious aggression problems, and could only think of one pathologically aggressive dog in her experience. The aggression had nothing to do with the dog's upbringing. The owner was experienced, the dog came from a good breeder and a well-balanced home. Most dogs give warning signals before biting, but there were none from this dog. She was an anomaly.

More often than not with reactive dogs, she simply saw owner and dog dysfunction. One dog in particular came to mind, a classic example of dog and owner working at cross-purposes. "He was the neatest dog," she recalled, "but he was confused by his owner's inconsistency. It got to the point where he'd run into a tunnel in the arena, and I couldn't get him out. Once he came to me and sat down in front of me, and he had this look on his face, like: Save me, save me! His handler was a lovely person. In fact, that might have been part of the problem. She hadn't been able to set boundaries for the dog."

Lois didn't believe every aspect of negative behaviour could be solved by reactive training. Negative checks had their place. "Dogs need to know when they do something wrong, and that can be signaled without resorting to force. You can mark the behaviours you don't want with something as simple as 'uh-uh.' I'd much rather have dogs working with me because they are willing partners than to avoid pain, or because they're afraid of me."

There is still some of the old punishment-based training around, and people sometimes show up to her agility classes with a six-month-old puppy wearing a pinch collar—simply unnecessary.

***

I joined the class on the last night of the reactive training course, not knowing what to expect. There was Max, Sweetie, Jake, Pix and George, in their respective corners with their respective owners. They were working on leash-walking this evening, doing the "toe line-up," as Lois called it—walking a few steps forward, then a half-turn to halt the dog, then another few steps before the dog got ahead, another half-turn, and lengthening each interval until the dog was effectively heeling.

And they were getting it. At least most of them were.

The atmosphere in the arena was no longer charged with panic. Max, the English sheepdog-wolfhound cross, was calmly sitting for treats. He had discovered the best way to get a reward was to sit down. Now, whenever he was uncertain about something, he simply sat. Lois approved; sitting was an excellent default for a dog like Max.

Bad-boy Jake was almost unrecognizable. For the first fifteen minutes I thought his handler had brought a different dog. Jake's eyes were glued to his mistress. And Sweetie was managing *not* to bark every single minute. Pix was listening much better—still towing his handler around the arena, but perhaps not quite so violently.

Unfortunately the little terrier, George, the growler, had not made much progress. George was a quick and determined little character, and his handlers—the second husband and wife team—looked very grim about the situation. The wife was clearly at her wits end as she tried to pull George around the arena. When Lois stepped in to demonstrate the dog became compliant—but only momentarily. As soon as his mistress took back the leash the terrier resumed his churlish behaviour.

The husband took over and simply ambled away, like he was going for a stroll by himself, dragging the dog behind. A better example of inconsistent approach couldn't be demonstrated. Other than this exception, I had no doubt I was seeing life-saving improvement for the rest.

Now—if only their people could keep it up.

15 ANIMAL SHELTERS

-If the problem reflects society, the solution must involve everyone-

The two Animal Protection Officers pulled into the alley, and saw they would have their work cut out: two Neapolitan mastiffs, one tied to a tree and one loose in the yard. The first officer grabbed a camera and got out of the van to photograph a hole in the yard's fence, while her partner headed to the house to talk to the complainant.

The first officer was behind the vehicle, adjusting the camera, when the male mastiff came bounding towards the fence. She stepped back just as the dog burst through the hole and landed where she had been standing.

She dropped the camera, threw up her arms and lunged forward, yelling at the dog. Startled, the mastiff leapt back, and then spun to face her. His body was tensed and there was no mistaking the menace in his stare. She had to summon all her nerve not to turn her back and flee.

He gathered himself to charge again, and when he did she was ready—and went on the offensive again. From the corner of her eye she saw her partner, frozen on the house steps. A short fence separated them. The female mastiff was barking and lunging at the end of the rope. In the alley the male mastiff attacked again. Again, she side-stepped and countered-menaced with her arms.

They kept up this dodging dance for what seemed like an eternity. Would her partner think to call the police? Never before had she considered calling the police to dispatch a dangerous dog.

Suddenly, inexplicably, the male mastiff turned and retreated through the hole in the fence. The female stopped barking. The two dogs now watched her from inside the yard. With her eyes on the dogs, she flew to the back of the van to retrieve the catch poles. They would have to try to separate the dogs.

Fast forward a dozen years. The tall well-groomed woman in heels is Tiffiny, former Animal Protection Officer and present Director of our local SPCA. In her twenty-two years with the shelter she has held many positions—and extricated herself from more jams than this one. The male mastiff, she told me, managed to break away and run a few blocks to a house where he used to live. There, after the dog attacked the door, a terrified family called 911. She believed he was trying to get inside to safety. She and her colleague were unable to get the dogs under control before the male mastiff injured himself. His behaviour wasn't typical of mastiffs, she assured me.

Less than five percent of the dogs taken in by the SPCA are considered dangerous. At the time I spoke to her the shelter was taking in almost 5,000 animals a year—about 1,500 dogs and twice as many cats. Almost 85% of the dogs were successfully homed or reclaimed by their owners, compared to only 45% of cats. "Of the dogs not homed, some have medical issues or are at the end of life. Or they have behaviour issues that we aren't able to resolve," Tiffiny said.

The SPCA doesn't euthanize dogs for space limitations, but if the City's Animal Control Department impound a dog involved in a human attack, and that impoundment results in a court order for destruction, the SPCA is responsible for that too. It's a dirty job and one that reflects badly on us all.

Tiffiny had brought to work that morning her own two Staffordshire terriers, Jasmine and Jersey, both adopted from the SPCA. Jersey was found in a parking lot beside a chain pet store and Jasmine was surrendered by an owner whose girlfriend was terrified of the breed. The two dogs were stretched out on the office floor. Jasmine kept up a gentle but steady demand for treats and Jersey a groaning commentary as he dozed.

"Staffordshires, like mastiffs, get a 'bad rap' for over-dominant and aggressive behaviour," said Tiffiny. "Certain breeds are considered 'status' breeds, meaning people tend to get them because they symbolize power. But they don't always put in the right training and socialization to make sure they are stable and sociable. People often fail to understand the dog's needs—those naturally occurring behaviours that must be met to prevent them from becoming frustrated and developing problematic behaviour."

Dangerous dogs are at the far end of the spectrum of problematic behaviour. Even poorly treated dogs don't usually pose a danger to anyone, she underscored. The rare dog that *does* pose a threat isn't necessarily doomed, thanks to important new city bylaws. Until recently, dangerous dog charges fell under the Urban Municipalities Act. Under the Act, an order for destruction was black and white: if a judge determined a dog to be dangerous there was an automatic destruction order. "If the judge *didn't* want to see the dog destroyed because of circumstances, then he couldn't declare it dangerous," Tiffiny said. "The City developed the bylaw to allow the judge to pick and choose what to do. Now, if the judge wants a confinement order, the provisions are included in that order and they proceed from there. So now, when we see a dangerous dog, the owner will have to carry out certain provisions to ensure the dog will be safe in the community and under their control at all times."

That change has meant an improvement in animal welfare locally. A dog involved in an attack isn't likely to go looking for another victim, she assured me. Dog bites are usually threat-specific, and unprovoked dog attacks on humans are very rare. With the exception of dogs with rage syndrome, a genetic disorder marked by an absence of escalating aggression signals, even abused dogs follow a clear pattern of warning.

"Dogs are very direct in their communication and they never do things accidentally," she said. "We sometimes hear people say, 'he almost bit me.' Well, if he didn't bite you, but he snapped at you, that's what he intended to do. There's a difference."

A dog's behaviour serves only to communicate, and if he's uncomfortable with a situation he lets you know. His first communication might be a rigid body, eye avoidance, or lip-licking. If the situation doesn't resolve he might take the warning up a notch to lip curling—barking, snarling, nipping or snapping—before a bite. "Every step of the way is intentional," said Tiffiny.

Tiffiny's path to working with the SPCA seemed pre-destined from a young age. As a child, she brought home stray animals, but her sister had allergies so the family couldn't keep any of the pets. "The strays always ended up with our neighbours," she said.

Shelter work involves more than finding homes for dogs and cats. Tiffiny studied animal behaviour to help control animals like the rampaging mastiff, and to be able to remove neglected animals during a seizure. "Understanding animal behaviour is key to reducing stress and injury in homeless animals," she said, "*especially* animals taken from poor home environments."

Tiffiny is an educator, a strategist, and a member of the Board of the Canadian Federation of Humane Societies. She also has the dubious distinction of having been vaccinated against potential rabies exposure no less than eight times.

What impact does a negative environment have on a dog's ability to cope later in life? "A distressed dog is going to respond differently than a secure dog," she replied. "Usually when we see a dog that isn't social or safe—one that we can't yet consider adopting out—it's either because that dog has had negative experiences in the past, or because the dog hasn't been exposed to certain things."

She explained that negative behaviour can escalate if a dog's fear or anxiety is not interpreted correctly, and pointed to the example of the mailman, that classic dog nemesis. "The mailman comes to the door, the dog barks, the mailman leaves—so the dog's communication seems effective. The next day, the mailman comes back. He didn't get the message. Most dogs are social enough that this doesn't become a serious problem, but we do see dogs that will escalate in aggression as the stimulus continues. The dog is trying to communicate to the mailman: 'I don't want you here, you left yesterday, why are you back?'"

As Lois pointed out earlier, misunderstood communication is often at the root of behavioural issues. Problem behaviour, even unexpected behaviour, is the number one reason people surrender animals to a shelter. "We deal with the animals that are cast off," Tiffiny stated. "It's unfortunate and it's wasteful. We see a lot of beautiful animals here. The system has failed—*we* have failed. People have not taken responsibility for their pets, and the shelters are to blame too, because we've enabled people to just leave them on our doorstep."

How do we foster better understanding of animal behaviour and encourage owners to take more responsibility? These are questions that SPCAs and other shelters have been trying to answer for years. "It is top of mind right now for the Federation of Humane Societies," she said. "Shelter numbers are still very high, and the rescue organizations have only relieved some of the pressure."

The Canadian Federation of Humane Societies (CFHS) gathers data on the number of animals entering, adopted, returned, or euthanized in Canadian shelters. In 2015, shelters took in over 82,000 cats and over 35,000 dogs. Almost *one third* of all the dogs were surrendered by their owners.

"That's one in every three dogs in the shelter, taken there by its *owner*," she underscored.

Unfortunately, some animals are repeatedly surrendered by the same people. SPCAs across North America are presently in the uncomfortable position of having to reconsider policies that allow people to continue surrendering animals. "It's a tough balance to maintain," Tiffiny said, "because no one wants to see animals in the community that are neglected."

One of the SPCAs' most difficult challenges is combatting the attitude that *this* particular dog or *this* special cat will have no trouble finding another home. "People say, 'This one is really cute, I know you'll find it a home.' Well," she declared, "we have a few hundred animals in our shelter that are also cute. We might have as many as eighty-five dogs and one hundred and fifty cats here at any given time. With dogs, the number fluctuates, but with cats it's pretty steady. So when people drop off an animal and say, 'You'll have no problem…'" She trailed off, clearly frustrated.

Of the 35,000 dogs taken into all Canadian animal shelters in 2015, about half were successfully adopted. A third of these were reclaimed by their owners (compared to just 5% of cats reclaimed), 8% were euthanized (compared to 19% of cats) and the remainder were transferred, died or remained in the shelter. Some good news is that the total intake of animals has decreased a bit, but that the decline may be made up for by the independent rescue agencies. Adoption rates for dogs have remained stable at about 50%—but adoption still makes up only about half the outcomes for shelter animals. (CFHS 2016)

When the CFHS first noted an increase in animal intake in 2008 the excess was linked to the economic recession. However, as Tiffiny pointed out, pets are a growth industry, and one that shows little sign of abating.

"It take resources to make dogs and cats adoptable," said Tiffiny. "There is a cost to providing pleasant viewing spaces for people to meet the animals—which is needed to rival pet stores. There is also a cost associated with programs like rehabilitative training, which is sometimes needed to make damaged animals adoptable."

They were currently developing a behaviour modification program with the intent of improving adoption rates. The objective was to tackle common behaviour problems, like resource guarding, that often prevent successful rehoming of dogs.

"With resource guarding," said Tiffiny, "certain objects or food items become of high value to the dog— like toys and blankets—things that were hard to come by in the past. The behaviour sometimes becomes generalized, so a dog can become very protective of an object. This is especially common in dogs denied regular feeding."

The idea behind the behaviour modification program is to avoid passing on problem behaviours to inexperienced owners. Ideally, the SPCA would be able to afford outreach services to help owners fix problems before they become so severe that the dog is surrendered.

Not that all dogs in shelters have behavioural problems. Most of them, in her view, have simply failed to meet the expectations of their owners. "The more information we have about an animal, the easier it is to make decisions about the appropriate placement—one that will be a success. Dogs that are cute and have some manners are not difficult to rehome, but, if you don't know a dog's background, chances are that the animal will be returned to the shelter. Something will pop up that the adopted family isn't prepared to take on."

I was curious to hear what she had learned about *people* during her years working at the shelter. She laughed, a little uneasily, and admitted that it was easier to talk about the animals than people.

"I love being able to teach staff and volunteers how to interact with the animals, and how to handle them properly. When working with the public, two things can happen: one, you can make a connection and a difference for an individual and an animal. Or two, they can totally disregard what you're trying to do and what you're saying, and you may end up having to take further action."

There *are* animals in the community that aren't in good home situations but circumstances are such that the SPCA cannot legally intervene. It might seem like a hopelessly stressful working situation but Tiffany could also appreciate that the shelter didn't always know the full story leading up to a seizure or surrender.

"Sometimes," she admitted, "shelter staff do become jaded towards the public. We experience the same kind of trauma as the police, paramedics or emergency room staff. We all deal with emotional trauma, and it just keeps coming, there's no 'down time.' We might have a lull, but our staff, like other welfare workers, must deal with compassion fatigue. You go through different emotions— you're angry, you're in despair, you're feeling helpless, or you want to save the world and make a difference. Sometimes you can be really, really down, and in a dark place."

Tiffany had been working on a staff development strategy to create small celebrations around successes. It was important, she believed, to focus on the positive impact shelters make in the lives of animals and people. "It's easy to think about all the failures," she admitted. "You come to work in the morning and think, I've got seventy cats to look after; maybe two will get adopted.

And then tomorrow maybe ten more cats will come in. But we don't think too much about the two cats that *did* get adopted today."

There *are* legitimate reasons for surrendering an animal to the SPCA. Knowing and accepting this has been an important coping mechanism for her. As she put it, "Circumstances are such that the animal is here. The person needs our help, they can't take care of their animal. Or we may be intervening because they haven't looked after the animal and haven't recognized that. We take steps to alleviate the situation, but we might not understand where that person has been."

She admitted that she was still learning to focus on one thing at a time, and to acknowledge daily that the shelter was only one piece of the puzzle of peoples' lives. "Whatever brought the animal here is all we can deal with right now. Whether or not the person is at fault or just a victim of circumstances we have to be mindful that we have a job to do, and do what we do best: look after the animal and make sure its needs are met."

The resilience of dogs was something that continued to inspire her. "Dogs don't dwell on things," she said, smiling. "They're the best examples we have of living in the 'here-and-now.' What are we doing, *today*? Dogs don't hold grudges—they *do* remember—but most of them will error on the side of trust. That's what I especially love about the Staffordshires."

Jersey and Jasmine, having come to the end of the treats, had both fallen asleep on the office floor. I found it hard to believe that anyone could abandon such beautiful dogs.

"When you have a bond with a Staffordshire," Tiffiny said, "it's strong. The Staffordshire terrier was bred for baiting badgers. Very tenacious, bold, and courageous. But they've also been known throughout history as the nanny dog, for their loyalty and bonding to the family. They're very protective of children and other animals."

Her first Staffordshire, Worf, an eighty-two pound American Staffordshire, was described once by her vet as "a person in a dog-suit raised by cats." Worf was goofy and jovial and loved people and animals—a true nanny dog. Tiffiny often brought home animals from the shelter that required some extra foster care, and Worf took his role as their protector seriously. He protected a litter of baby hedgehogs; he allowed a parrot to climb on him and preen his feet; he permitted a little boxer with resource guarding issues to guard the whole kitchen—he wasn't concerned about his own food.

Towards the end of my visit Tiffiny showed me around the shelter. We started with a couple of success stories. Two purebred boxers, brother and sister, greeted us energetically in a small and pleasant viewing room. They had been abandoned eight months ago, and no one would guess how severely emaciated they had been when they were found. They had not only lost fat and muscle tissue but bone density and organ tissue. Food had to be re-introduced slowly, and the survival of one had been uncertain for weeks. Today, they were literally bouncing with good health.

"To see these dogs, after being neglected like that," Tiffiny broke off. "You know what? This is a good place to be."

The corridors of the shelter were spotless. We passed a young worker who was scouring the walkways and walls with a mop and hose, a daily routine. The presence of plush animals and stuffed toys added some cheer to the rooms, but it was hard to escape the fact that this was an institution of depressing permanence.

Animal shelters are the sentinels of human failure, the dark side of ourselves. Long after we had been through the adoption rooms, through Incoming Assessment, Isolation, Cats and Exotics, and the supply room (one wall stocked with donated feed to share with other rescue organizations), long after we paused against a door that was covered with hundreds of leashes and collars, the individual dogs in the shelter would haunt me.

The boxer puppies, the Australian shepherd that leapt continuously (literally climbing his kennel walls), the black Lab found by the highway. The Lab sat so still in the midst of the cacophony of barking—forty-eight hours, he'd been in the pound, and another twenty-four to go before his owners lost the right to reclaim him.

Tiffiny believed, and I had to agree, that the problem of homeless animals was much broader than a matter of irresponsible pet-owners and inadequate shelter resources. The problem reflected a whole society—an unflattering self-image—and therefore the solution must involve everyone.

"It will require the pet owners, non-pet owners, veterinarians, everybody that is involved, to solve the problem of over-crowded shelters," said Tiffiny. "We've domesticated these animals and we're responsible for them."

Tiffiny mentioned that the staff were very much cheered by successful adoption stories and welcomed drop-ins from former adoptees. I took Tove in one morning to visit. There had been a turnover in staff since his particular seizure, but at least one shelter worker remembered it well enough to appreciate Tove's recovery.

It was Christmas time, and there were cards from grateful families plastered to the walls of the shelter. A reception desk overflowed with gift boxes of chocolates and other goodies from SPCA supporters. Tiffiny and another staff member were chatting with me near the front door when a man came in and held out an envelope.

"I just wanted to drop off this card," he said, shyly. "We adopted a dog from here about a year ago. I wanted to tell you that he's fine, and to give you this photo. He's really doing well."

16 END OF LIFE

-The miracle of life is the joy and intensity of living-

Liam, Tove and I arrived in Banff in a snowstorm, a flurry of snowflakes, greetings and Christmas parcels. My friend J.J. and the indefatigable Jersey, her shepherd-husky cross, met us at the door. Steve, J.J.'s husband, and their son, Emmett, helped to unload the car, and, in the midst of the commotion, Tove committed his first *faux pas* as a house guest; he lifted his leg on the Christmas tree. J.J. screeched, Jersey barked with indignation, and Steve leapt to rescue the presents.

Jersey was looking a bit more decrepit than the last time I saw her. She was only eight years old but looked older, her face whitened and her gait stiff. She'd been diagnosed with an inoperable tumor in October, and was thought unlikely to live into the new year. As December approached I'd been worried that spending Christmas with J.J. and her family would be too much for Jersey—what with Tove along with us, and the usual Christmas discombobulation. But J.J. had insisted; the boys were looking forward to skiing, J.J. and I would cook, Steve and

I would cross-country ski, and we'd all play Mexican rummy and sing carols in the evenings. In between, we'd walk the dogs along the Bow River. It would be the perfect Christmas.

Tove instantly understood his place in the mix: Jersey was top dog. Tove might outsize and outrun her but Jersey's seniority clearly ranked her as the alpha dog. Tove's presence seemed to perk Jersey up and made her forget her arthritis. She stalked around the house, throwing meaningful glances in Tove's direction, and then took up her usual post on the landing near the front door—the better to keep an eye on the comings and goings of the household.

Tove took the hint and retreated to the basement. We left the two of them to sort it out and got on with the jolly business of making Christmas. When it was time for a walk J.J. told us to go ahead because Jersey couldn't go very far. "We'll meet you on Deer Street on your way back," she said.

Liam and I headed up the mountain path from the house with Tove pulling eagerly at the lead. A few hundred meters up the slope we stepped almost directly into the path of a magnificent elk. Tove was so stunned by its size that he stood shock still. A small group of doe elk grazed a dozen feet from the trail, and we watched them for a while before turning back.

At the bottom of Deer Street Jersey lay at J.J.'s feet. J.J. was on her cell phone. Jersey thumped her tail on the snowy pavement as we approached but she didn't get up. "C'mon Emmett, pick up," J.J. muttered. When I asked her what was wrong she said Jersey couldn't get up. "Can we carry her?" Liam asked. J.J. shook her head. Emmett would come. Emmett knew how to carry her without hurting her.

***

If anyone is instantly recognizable as a dog person it's my friend J.J. A post card tacked to her office door describes her perfectly: "Warning: occupant subject to unrestrained bursts of enthusiasm." She is the only person I know who stops to greet every single dog she meets on the street.

Jersey was put down shortly after our Christmas visit. The following Christmas, almost exactly one year later, our two families got together again. By now a new dog had joined the household: Ringo, another shepherd-husky cross. Ringo was smaller and leaner than Jersey, and, like Jersey, a rescue dog from the North. He was not quite a year old, and this time Tove took up the alpha position in the house.

Tove lorded his seniority and superior size. Ringo did not challenge him. He was a bright, skittish youngster and didn't complain—even when Tove took his chew bone. Clearly, the pup had become the apple of J.J.'s eye. I was glad to see that she had recovered from Jersey's death. It had been terribly hard for her to lose Jersey.

When I asked her what she liked most about Ringo she said he was very attentive. Most of the time he seemed to prefer her company to the rest of the family. He was a bit more independent than Jersey but he came to her when she called. "At first he wasn't very good about that, but this past summer, after we spent time by ourselves, he started to understand that he and I were the main relationship."

Being chosen—being the one the dog wants to be with—has always been important to J.J.. Her childhood was turbulent, "emotionally chaotic," as she put it. She remembered as a little girl going to lie down with the dogs on their dog beds. Just to be near them was comforting.

Having suffered all her life from anxiety she thought a kind of dependency on dogs may have developed. I could identify with this myself, as I had developed something of a dependency on Tove. In almost any social setting I found his presence reassuring. It would be easy to become dependent on him for companionship.

Jersey had been part of J.J. and her family's life for eight years—more than half of Emmett's lifetime. I had been thinking for a while about this difficult chapter in every dog owner's life—losing a beloved companion—and I was perplexed by how quickly our beloved dogs are often replaced. I didn't doubt the sincerity of the attachment or the grief of loss, but how does a new pet inveigle its way so quickly into our hearts? Another friend of mine had recently lost her much-loved shepherd of many years, and within weeks had found another dog, reminiscent of her old friend.

I myself was no stranger to the phenomenon. Liam and I both were bereft when our family cat of thirteen years had to be put down. Yet within two months, a new kitten was commanding our affections. Was this conspicuous evidence of the frailty of human loyalty?

Jersey's death was still painful for J.J. to talk about, but she and I have been friends for a long time and she was ready to talk about it. We had been walking the dogs that afternoon, and when we returned we took our coffee into the living room. The boys and Steve were out. The snow was falling on the mountains and the lights twinkled on the streets. It was peaceful, and as good a time as any to talk about losing Jersey.

Jersey was not the first dog J.J. had to put down. She'd made that decision for Baxter, her flat-coated retriever, about eight years before. I remembered Baxter well because I'd looked after him a few times when J.J. and Steve were away, before the boys were born. He was a big unwieldy character with a very intense nature, and his need for attention was both touching and overwhelming. Baxter liked physical contact. He liked to be close. I remembered how he would try to curl up against me in bed, as solid and immovable as a wall.

Baxter could be *too* clingy, J.J. admitted. "He wanted to please me so much that when Emmett was born his heart was broken. He followed us around endlessly. He was so desperate, so worried. It was like he had an existential crisis. One day he went out in the back yard and pulled all the tomatoes off the plants. He lay down, way at the back of the property. I mean, really had a breakdown. He was really *really* dependent on me. Much more than I wanted him to be. Poor old Baxter."

She regretted keeping Baxter going for too long after it was time to let him go. Baxter, like Jersey, developed cancer before he was eight years old. He had a lot of veterinary care in his short lifetime, including surgery for a twisted bowel and a hip replacement. He also had arthritis, and the drugs cost a fortune. A fortune gladly spent, she added, but, in the end, an enlarged heart and lung cancer would finish him. His life could not be extended.

It wasn't that she had trouble with euthanasia—in fact, just the opposite. "I think it's wonderful that we can help them in a way that we can't get our heads around helping ourselves. I thought I'd just *know* when it was time to put him down. I tried intellectually to read the signs."

People would sometimes say things to J.J. like, "Look at that poor old dog, he can hardly get down the ramp." At first, J.J. didn't see it or didn't *want* to see it. Finally, when the vet said there was nothing more they could do for him, she decided, there on the spot. "Well, take him, then," she said.

Tove and Ringo were dozing peacefully at our feet, and I felt a sadness open up between J.J. and me. In moments when I face the eventuality of losing Tove, I think there can be no way to prepare for that final day.

J.J. confirmed precisely that—losing Baxter had not helped her to prepare to lose Jersey. Both dogs, right up to the end, still had a lust for life. Perhaps part of her reluctance to let go was not wanting to give up on a faithful friend.

Another thing that made the decision difficult for her was the fact that the end of life isn't one continual and painful decline. "Good days follow bad," she said. "One good day, three bad, two good—and how can you tell how long the good or the bad will last? With some things it *was* a steady decline. I thought Jersey would gradually get sicker and sicker and then I'd help her out the door. But that wasn't all there was to it. "

I could see how easy it would be to avoid, even deny, the inevitable. Jersey had always *been there*; she was in every family photo, she was under the dining table, underfoot in the kitchen, greeting people at the door with her funny "roo." She got a lot of enjoyment out of life and she shared that enthusiasm. The joy of a dog is so obvious— the appetite for a treat, the luxurious tummy rub, the tennis ball coming out of a pocket. So many tender details, so much shared history.

J.J. was silent. And then, "You know, putting a dog down is hard because the dog doesn't want to be put down. They look at you, and they just want to be with you, no matter what. They don't care about aches and pains, they'll put up with it all. And in the end you have to say, 'No, you can't live this way.'"

I asked her if she thought that the reluctance to let go had anything to do with our *own* needs. "Putting our own needs first, you mean?" she said, but then, "No, I consciously tried to put the dog's suffering ahead of my own selfishness, because I've seen others do that. I don't know why people can't let them go if it's clear the time has come. Say five friends come to you and say, 'You really should let your dog go.' If you don't or can't listen, if you're really in that much in denial, then it's about something else."

She opened her laptop on the coffee table to show me some pictures of Jersey that were taken last Christmas. In one of them Jersey wore a Santa cape and fuzzy antlers. "When I discovered these, it was just so wonderful to see her again. Look, she's looking right at me. And I'm looking at her. We loved each other," she said. "We *loved* each other."

A few moments passed while she studied the picture, and then she said, "I think Ringo and I love each other now, but I didn't love him at first, you know. I remember, with both Ringo and Jersey, thinking, 'I don't think I can love this dog. I don't feel the connection.' With both of them, it took time."

There is something elusive about our partnership with dogs. Part of me wants the connection to be unique. When the time comes, as it eventually will, part of me wants Tove to be irreplaceable. In writing about dogs and talking to people about them, in getting to know the different breeds and different roles, I still struggle to capture the essence of that relationship. Words may describe the dog, the dog's purpose, the skills of the dog, the behavioural nuts and bolts. But to live closely with an animal, to recognize the specialness of that interaction is—not exactly to see life through different eyes, but to glimpse something truly valuable.

Woven into that experience are the threads of an understanding that becomes a kind of consciousness. *These* are the ties that binds us, this heightened awareness. This sliver of shared knowledge.

I once read about a young man who found himself waiting for the right time to end his old dog's life. The dog had been failing for some time. The man led his dog down a boulevard one day and helped the dog to relieve himself. The dog had become so crippled that he couldn't crouch, so the man had to hold him up. A pickup truck passed them, braked and pulled over. An older man got out and came over. "I'm sorry," he said, "but I just had to stop when I saw you. I wanted to tell you, because I've been here myself. You need to know. It's time."

Many dog owners talk about this final duty we perform for our dogs, done from love and a sense of responsibility. As one person pointed out, part of the difficulty is that this is a choice we make only for our pets. It is unusual, even counter-intuitive, to make this decision to end life.

When the time to end Jersey's life drew near, Emmett said he wanted to be there. He'd been upset about not being with Baxter. "I hadn't really considered that back then," said J.J. "I just thought, 'Well, *I* have to do this, this is *my* dog.'"

She described Jersey's last day plainly. "The vet and the assistant came to the house. When everything was prepared the vet said, 'All right, I have the needle ready,' and then, 'Okay, I'm going to give her the injection.' Every step of the procedure we knew what was happening. Jersey was on the landing on her blanket, in her usual spot. I was on the first step with her, and Emmett and Steven were behind. I was just stroking her head, and she was looking at me, kind of like, 'What's going on?' But she was *there*, connected with us. And it was *so* fast—you can't even say it was a split second. It was like a puff of breath, and she was gone."

Ringo stirred on the floor at our feet. I wiped my eyes. J.J. was looking at Ringo with affection. I knew her fondness for the pup was mixed with remembering Jersey. I thought to myself, so this is it: the miracle of loss. Intensified living.

J.J. explained it more simply.

"When you have a tendency towards anxiety, like I do, and you worry about things before and after the fact—instead of just being in the present—the dog is a very good reminder of the *right now*. Right now means, 'Hey, aren't we going for a walk?' That's what matters."

Ringo and Tove pricked up their ears at the word "walk."

J.J. and I laughed, but it was bittersweet. As much as they remind us of the here-and-now, dogs remind us that what we share in this world is temporary.

"But," as J.J. put it, "if you didn't have them, you wouldn't love them. And you get to be with them for their whole lives. *That* really is something. Being with a dog for its whole life! For Baxter's life, and Jersey's life, and now for Ringo's whole life! That's a wonderful gift."

Getting a new dog after losing an old friend may just be about sharing another life. Certainly there is something rare in a dog that wants to be with you—*you*, above all others, a companion to follow you everywhere and anywhere.

Perhaps our tendency to replace our beloved dogs comes from the urge to connect and reconnect, to love and be loved.

Be that as it may, I was left with the lingering image of Emmett, as he carried Jersey home last Christmas. Emmett, whom I had known from the time he was a baby, now a tall and lanky teenager. The way he ran down the road toward us in his shirtsleeves, how he tenderly scooped up the dog and carried her home in his arms. Walking ahead of us, in silent distress.

17 A VET'S VIEW

-Dogs are not people-

When nine-year-old Keziah and her mother arrived at the vet clinic the technician, Linda, was assembling the surgery packs. Keziah gathered up the clean towels and put them on the heating-pad on the stainless steel table. The lady with the pregnant dog arrived and her mother examined the dog. The Lab had been trying to whelp for four hours—still no puppies. Her mother said the dog's discharge meant the placentas were separating. "I think I can feel four or five pups," she said. "There may be one blocking the pelvis."

They were going to perform a Cesarean section. Keziah washed her hands and found a clean lab coat while her mother scrubbed for surgery. The white lab coat was too big for her and reached down to her ankles. She stationed herself in the doorway of the surgery suite and watched her mother, gowned, gloved and masked, open up the Labrador's belly and then the uterus.

Keziah was used to accompanying her mother to the vet clinic once or twice a month when she was on call. She liked to help check the intravenous lines, to clean up the patients and walk the dogs. Unlike her younger sister, she wasn't the least bit squeamish about surgeries.

In a few minutes her mother was handing the first pup to Linda, and Keziah followed on her heels to the treatment room. "Like this," Linda said, after stripping off the sticky-looking amniotic sac, rubbing the puppy's rib cage in a circular motion. Keziah took the cool limp pup and held it firmly on the warm towel. The pup wriggled weakly and opened its mouth. Linda drew the hose from the oxygen machine and put the dome over the pup's nose. Keziah held the mask in one hand and kept up the rhythmic stroking with the other. She knew this helped the puppies to breath.

The pup on the table was starting to "pink-up." Linda was soon back with the second pup. The owner of the dog now joined them, and Keziah showed her how to rub the first pup so that she could take the second pup from Linda. In thirty minutes there were five puppies lined up on the towels: two females and three males—all they could comfortably handle with three sets of hands.

Her mother leaned into the room to ask how the pups were doing. Each little mouth was a healthy pink. Keziah reported they would not lose a single pup.

I wish I could say that I witnessed this little miracle first-hand, but I had to reconstruct it from Becky's description. Becky is our family veterinarian, whom I have known since university. When I was Keziah's age I was fortunate enough to witness our hunting dog, Mutz, whelp a litter of nine pups. I can't think of anything I'd have loved more than to assist in a real veterinary procedure like this one.

Too many children are guarded from witnessing animal birth, which is a formative experience: a new living creature enters the world, totally dependent on its mother and the environment. Though Keziah may have been too young to fully appreciate the significance of her role, I'm certain the memory of the event will stay with her for a lifetime.

One afternoon in early September, Becky, Keziah and their handsome husky-greyhound cross, Booker, visited Tove and I in our backyard. Keziah would be starting grade four in a few days. She had two younger siblings at home: a seven-year-old sister and a brother who was four. Her dad was a teacher, and she told me that she was planning to be a teacher in the winter time and a vet in the summer.

"Can you speak dog?" I asked Keziah. "What do you suppose they're saying to one another?" Tove and Booker were performing the doggie meet-and-greet on our porch, and negotiating their relative status. "They're greeting each other," she said, solemnly. "They want to talk to each other so they sniff to each other."

Keziah struck me as a quietly confident youngster. When I asked her about her pets at home she told me she couldn't remember a time when they didn't have a dog. Booker was one of several animals at home. "We have two cats, four gerbils, three fish and one rabbit," she said. "I feed the gerbils. Sometimes they bite, but it doesn't hurt. Booker is an only dog."

There is something basic about children and puppies growing up together, something fundamental to the nurturing process. Becky told me that she'd known from an early age she was going to be a vet. Growing up next door to her uncle's dairy farm in Manitoba, her vocation was, as she put it, "served up on a plate." It didn't necessarily follow that Keziah would take the same path, but Becky intended to provide the opportunity for each of her three children.

Becky had been in veterinary practice now for more than ten years, and I can personally vouch that this small slender woman is as rugged as she is versatile. In addition to her regular veterinary practice, she performs animal acupuncture for the treatment of chronic pain and animal infertility. When I asked her what practicing vet medicine was like she said, "Your training is just the beginning. You get out there and you realize how much you *don't* know. You may learn about animals, but you don't learn about people."

That being said, one of the things she most enjoyed about veterinary practice was building relationships with her human clients. "You become a little bit like part of the family in some circumstances," she said. "Generally, everyone's heart is in the right place. Some people have more knowledge than others, but there are very few people who bring their pet into the clinic who don't want to help their animal."

Veterinarians have a unique view of the world, with an rare understanding of animals and a solid grounding in human affairs. The vets I've known over the years have been practical, down-to-earth individuals, short on sentimentality and long on patience. They also have a special brand of humour—which likely comes with the territory. The last time I took Tove to the clinic we were sitting in the waiting room when we heard a commotion coming from one of the examining rooms. A little dog Becky was examining became so nervous it peed in its mistress's purse. The owner didn't think it was so funny. Everyone in the waiting room, hearing her shrieks through the wall, was in stitches.

"She was *so* mad!" Becky chuckled, recalling it. She admitted she probably saw people and their animals at their best and at their worst. "There are always challenging cases and challenging people," she said.

In addition to her regular clinic clients she occasionally saw some of the shelter dogs. "The abuse and neglect cases are relatively rare, but yes, they *are* hard to get your head around. Lots of times it's because of lack of knowledge on the part of the owner—they just don't know any better. At least you try to give them the benefit of the doubt."

For Becky, the hardest part about veterinary practice is the more common occurrence when people can't afford, or don't want to spend money for proper medical workup. An ounce of prevention is worth costly and painful intervention later on, in her view.

I asked her what it took, emotionally, to euthanize animals as part of her routine work. "You develop a bedside manner," she said. "You have to, or you'd be torn apart every time. Euthanasia doesn't bother me too much, especially when it's an older sick pet, because it's one of the kindest things we're able to do for them. You tell people that it's one of the hardest decisions they'll ever make, and even though they're making the right decision, they will always second-guess themselves. That's the nature of euthanasia."

She occasionally met people who wanted to put an animal down when that wasn't necessary. "That's a tough one," she said. "In some cases, it's just a matter of convenience for the owner. You try to steer them in another direction. If that doesn't work, people will sometimes surrender the animal to the clinic, sign it over, so the clinic absorbs the cost of the procedure and will find someone to take care of the animal. Luckily it doesn't happen too often."

At the other end of the caring spectrum are pet owners who develop an unhealthy dependency on their pet. "There are times when a dog is clearly a surrogate spouse or child," she said. "The pet really becomes an obsession, and it's not a healthy relationship."

Becky grew up with a clear understanding of the division between animals and people. People with working animals generally *get* the distinction, she told me. But in a world where fewer and fewer people have contact with working animals that distinction sometimes becomes blurred.

"If I had one thing to say to new dog owners," she said, "it would be to treat them as a dog, not a person."

Too much mutual dependency is hard on dogs—a fact borne out by trainers like Lois, who have seen the negative impact people can have on their pets. Becky added that we put a lot of pressure on dogs. "Most of us are at work all day and expect well-behaved companions when we get home."

The modern dilemma of urban dogs being locked up for long hours in apartments and houses means a lot of inactive waiting for dogs, a relatively new requirement in their long evolutionary history. The biggest issue between owners and dogs, in her view, is misunderstanding dog communication. "People don't pick up on how a dog behaves when it is stressed."

Jill Hornby, in the *Latchkey Dog*, wrote about the subtle cues we sometimes give our dogs that reinforce their insecurity. That insecurity also teaches them to depend upon our emotional well-being. The naughty dog seeks attention by resorting to bad behaviour because it is the only attention he can control. Almost overnight, the owner becomes "trained" to react in a certain way.

Dysfunctional, yes. Irreversible, no—though these dogs and their owners may need professional help. Manners are often the first thing to go when there is miscommunication. Not all misbehaviour, Becky acknowledged, is the fault of the owner, but she saw a lot of "out-of-control" dogs at the clinic. "If you look at the psychological issues that people have, animals have them too. In some cases, I don't know how people can have the dog in their home, because it's not safe with young children. Any dog has the potential to bite; if you're not reading the behaviour or understanding where the warning is...."

As if to prove her point, Booker and Tove suddenly developed mutual tensions. They had managed to wedge themselves beside Keziah, who was quietly munching cookies. Booker stood close to Tove—too close for his liking—and Tove rumbled. "Don't touch him, Keziah,"

Becky said calmly, "give him his space." Keziah held still, and in a few seconds the tensions passed, and the situation was resolved by the well-socialized Booker turning to investigate the garden.

Tove hopped up into a basket chair in a corner of the porch—that too was a statement. Later, I reflected on the fact that Becky didn't rely on Keziah's experience with dogs to pick up on Tove's warning. Keziah knew what a growling dog meant, but she still learned best through a warning from her mom.

Dog communication, I was learning, does not translate as easily as we might think, considering our long exposure to dogs. The fact is that humans communicate differently than dogs and have quite different learning strategies. The way we commit things to memory differs, and our information cues are dissimilar. The things we do poorly compared to dogs are too many to list—hence our long-time dependence on them—but we humans do pride ourselves in our communication skills.

I was only now beginning to understand some of the canine behaviours I'd been seeing all my life. I could now see these behaviours as distinct statements—but that wasn't thanks to my new-found powers of observation. Instead, I had internalized the contents of books and matched this knowledge to my observations—after the fact.

Growing up with family dogs, I had never learned, for example, that a dog climbs up high in order to mark seniority or rank. In spite of having spent over a year of *consciously* trying to understand dog behaviour, I was learning these things only lately, from other *people*.

As obvious as it should have been, it was only after my conversation with Becky and Keziah that I realized an important truth: we may learn what we live, and dogs have much to teach us, but primarily we learn from people.

***

Dr Marty Becker, an American veterinarian and popular talk-show guest, described how pets teach us how to form healthy human relationships. He noted that a child's first lesson in responsibility and sensitivity to the needs of others often comes from the family pet. He pointed to research that suggests that children and adolescents who are pet owners are more likely to report higher levels of well-being, self-reliance, self-control, and empathy, compared to non-pet-owning children.

Positive self-identity comes from the interactions that make us feel good about ourselves. Becker and other dog-book writers have suggested that the bonds we form, whether with people or other animals, are what make us truly human. The ties of friendship, dependence, trust and responsibility are the ties that keep us strong and resilient. It is no coincidence that the elements ideal for raising children—structure, consistency, kindness—are also the best conditions for fostering well-adjusted, well-mannered dogs.

It is tempting to assume that pets give us a healthy start in life but, as psychologists point out, it's hard to say whether pets encourage nurturing behaviour in children, or the families where pets live encourage nurturing behaviour in their children. Becky recognized a number of similarities between child-rearing and dog-rearing. "Discipline is one similarity," she said. "Both kids and dogs need boundaries. They have both taught me a lot about patience. I also think it's valuable for kids to have a pet. Being responsible for another living creature, one that is totally dependent on you, is important. That, and being respectful of them."

Booker had very much bonded to Becky. He came from the veterinary college kennels. "He was supposed to be used for a research project, but they had too many dogs so he went to Medical Exercises—that's where the third and fourth year vet students do non-invasive work. They practice physicals, learn to do blood tests, that kind of thing. They have five or six medical exercise dogs every year, and then re-home them after a year. Usually they have greyhounds for the blood donor clinic and keep them a year or two before re-homing them. Physically, they're fine, but they're kenneled—exercised, but it's not the same. Booker was kenneled, and he was a wild thing when he came to us."

I asked her if the veterinary world took a stand on the subject of purebred dogs. "I don't think there's any consensus in North America," she replied. "People *talk* about the problems in the brachiocephalic breeds—breeds with pushed-in faces, like bull-dogs—and those dogs really *do* have a hard time breathing—but there's little action to show for it. As far as cosmetic pedigree surgeries go, things like ear-cropping are opposed by lots of vets. It's illegal to perform ear cropping in most provinces now. We still do tail-docking within three days of birth. I expect that will end soon, and I'll have no problem with that. Declawing is a growing trend, unfortunately—it's an issue for cats. Europeans seem to be more progressive in terms of animal welfare than we are here."

As far as purebreds versus mixed breeds go, mixed breeds have always been popular as pets, she noted. But the rescue dog *is* becoming more popular, in her view. Veterinary colleges send teams of practicing students to communities with poor breeding control to perform neutering, but there would be no shortage of dogs needing rescue in the short term.

As distracted as Booker was—having to keep track of his mistress *and* Keziah in the presence of a strange dog, *and* with a strange garden beckoning—he gave me some friendly attention during our visit. He definitely had the husky energy. Becky described him as being very loyal. He had some hip dysplasia, so she kept his weight down to protect his joints ("People always think dogs that are a healthy weight look too thin. We're used to seeing overweight dogs," she commented). Booker suffered from separation anxiety. In the past, he used to accompany her to work, but now he stayed home in the garage when the family wasn't home, where he had a bed and a few toys and couldn't get into too much trouble.

"What's special to you about Booker?" I asked Keziah. "I like to play with him," she said. "We have a tube toy that we throw, and he fetches it. We have to wrestle him to get it."

She also thought Booker wasn't as smart as her friends' dogs because he didn't do "obedience stuff." I asked her what a smart dog does. "Follows you around and barks when you do something wrong?" she replied— more of a question. "I could use one of those," her mother laughed.

Becky admitted that she hadn't spent a lot of time on obedience with Booker. "Some breeds love obedience, and obedience becomes like a replacement job. A certain personality of dog performs obedience very well. But for some breeds obedience training just isn't the way they learn. Obedience is important to keep dogs and people safe, but the very precise stuff? I think basic manners are more important. Lots of people don't really want dogs to be dogs," she observed.

What about people and their dogs? She must have seen every possible combination. Did certain types of people tend to have certain breeds of dog? "Oh definitely," she answered. "Hunting dogs, like Labs, their people are very matter-of-fact. Small dogs are sometimes like a replacement child. German shepherd owners tend to be very no-nonsense. Sometimes similar interests bring dogs and people together – sports dogs and sports enthusiasts. Beyond that? Generalizations? Not so much."

When I asked Keziah what Booker had taught her, she looked puzzled by the question. Fair enough; the question had perplexed more than a few adults. I was coming to the conclusion that we don't really think about what we learn, or where we learn things. Many of life's lessons seem to come to us slowly, and insight develops over time.

I tried another tact with Keziah. "We teach dogs lots of things, like *come* and *sit* and *heel*—or we try. What do the dogs teach *us*?"

She answered me plainly. "They teach us about dogs. About their selves."

Her mother summed it up slightly differently. "We can certainly see ourselves in dogs. We're very similar when it comes right down to it. Biologically, physiologically, we're the same. We're put together the same way, and emotionally we're very similar too."

Similar, but not the same. It was an important distinction. I would have to consider the implications of this more fully.

18 WHAT WE LEARN

-Dogs do speak, but only to those who know how to listen-

What do we learn from dogs? Do we learn different lessons from different breeds? Do people with hunting dogs learn something different from people with herding dogs? If we were to take a score of individuals and give them the same experience, each would tell a different story: different details, similar meaning.

Most of the lessons shared in these chapters were common across all the breeds, but on some level there were unique truths. The dogs themselves share more commonalities than differences. Police dogs and therapy dogs share a sensitivity to interpersonal communication; hunters and herders share an understanding of intention. I did *not* find common personalities among owners of specific breeds—bull-dog owners *can* be non-game players, shepherd owners will *not* do absolutely anything for their friends, and although I didn't meet any dachshunds, I doubt *all* their people are bossy.

As to whether or not certain types of people are drawn to certain breeds, the answer lies somewhere between maybe and yes. General interests sometimes dictate our selection, and size suggests whether the dog is a lap-warmer or for protection. But, more often, serendipity rules the day.

What we personally gain from our experience with dogs has a lot to do with what we are prepared to learn about ourselves. I'm amazed at my early lack of knowledge about dog behaviour—in spite of having lifelong proximity to dogs. It is stunning to think that humankind has enjoyed the company of dogs for 140 centuries or more, that one in five households in North America today owns a dog, yet most of us never ask what their behaviour means.

I have learned a lot from the dogs and from the people I met since writing the first chapter. I have learned much to explain Tove's early behaviour. Some of his quirks are doubtless breed-dependent and some stem from his upbringing and early circumstances. The transition from pack life in a rural setting to a citified leash-bound existence took almost two years, and even now he continues to change in subtle ways.

He still occasionally sits down on the sidewalk and won't budge—usually, when he's trying to communicate a point.

Over the course of my inquiry I came to understand that dog people are connected to one another in unique ways. There is an underground of accessible knowledge out there; if you plug in at one point the network loops back to certain connections and certain individuals. People introduced me to people and for that I am grateful. Those I spoke to, with their different levels of knowledge and experience, did not think they were sharing wisdom with me. Wisdom isn't something easily translated—wise words aren't conscientiously gathered. In the beginning I thought I was trying to rehabilitate Tove and learn about different dog breeds along the way. Only later did I notice that much of what people learn from dogs is also valuable advice for living.

We have benefited from the work of dogs and from their companionship. We have manipulated their genes to suit our needs and largely taken their place by our side for granted. What, collectively, have we learned?

Dogs make us better people by revealing us to ourselves. Little has been said about discipline in these chapters. We all know that it is wrong to strike a dog in anger but most of us have done it at least once. As one individual told me, "It made me question myself as a human being."

The most common lessons that people repeated had to do with growing patience, increasing trust and the importance of consistency in relationships. The other most common message was that dogs help us to live in the here-and-now.

Here are a few more things that I learned personally.

Communication doesn't require a shared verbal language. Language is complex, and human relationships more so, but the world is more complex than we have language to describe anyway. Dogs help us to keep it simple.

Living peacefully and successfully with a dog isn't just a matter of personality matching; temperaments blend and mold to one another over time when we are generous and pay attention to *intention.*

When a dog chooses you it is high praise indeed. It is a gift of immeasurable value to be accepted as you are. Love, any love, makes us stronger and keeps us healthy. I get a deep belly laugh at least once a week from observing something Tove does, and a smile every day. A hundred sunrises and a thousand sunsets would have escaped my notice had there not been a reason to rise early, and *to linger.*

Bonding is a connection that runs deeper than love that sometimes requires self-discipline—a bit like succeeding in an arranged marriage. Bonding takes patience, tolerance, forgiveness, optimism, and the suspension of doubt. Most of all, bonding implies a willingness to be changed over time.

Dogs change. People change. We are sometimes motivated to change when we learn something truly important about ourselves. Tove went from being a recluse to a confirmed cuddler, all on the assumption that the world wasn't so bad after all. He learned to trust. He learned to eat from a dish and drink from a bowl. He has become a permanent fixture on my bed and gradually turned my ritual of the morning cup of tea to a mutual survey of the coming day, companionably curled together.

Food is love. Every little bit of sharing is an act of grace. I have learned not to get caught up in theories of dominance or having to prove something at feeding time. I feed Tove *before* we eat because it's convenient, and I always save one bite from my plate for him (into his dog dish so we don't get into the begging game). It reinforces that we are in this world together, and reassures him that I will take care of him.

Dogs have taught me the value of time. Spending time together is all anyone who loves us really wants from us. Slowing down, too, gives a wealth of health benefits and underscores the pleasures of the moment.

I've learned that obedience isn't everything and that the dog has, and should have, a mind of its own. Cooperation, manners and mutual respect trump blind obedience any day. Letting go is perhaps the most important lesson that I learned from Tove. Control isn't and shouldn't be everything—we *don't* and *can't* control everything. This is as it should be.

Confidence-building is big. Self-awareness, leadership, and kindness are big too. We ought to learn from one another, we ought to care for one another. We are part of a human pack.

Cat people have a lot to learn about dogs. I have some friends who are cat people whom Tove is slowly charming. He hasn't quite been admitted to their circle as an honorary cat, but they admit he is far from being the sloppy, noisy, shallow caricature of a dog that many cat people love to hate. It may be endearing to see dogs as unfocused, enthusiastic, sometimes gross, always needy—the idiotic cartoon Odie or Oatmeal—but the dogs I've met are far from being two-dimensional characters. If we think a dog's only purpose is to meet human emotional needs—be of good cheer, take nothing seriously, and above all just *be there*—we shouldn't expect more than a shallow understanding.

We should teach a child, teach an adult, how to greet a dog and to show respect. The world needs more dog knowledge and could always use more inter-species respect. When we respect others' needs and differences we grow personally.

There are lots of books on dog-speak, and a little knowledge of behaviour goes a long way when it is shared person-to-person. Tell your grouchy neighbour that garbage cans in the alley get marked because they're being marked by other animals. Let your children know that hugging a strange dog is a threatening gesture.

Also, share with the world that a growl is not a bite. It's a warning. There's a difference.

Let the dog be the whole dog. This has something to do with "letting go" and the notion of having to be in control. Let me be clear: dogs need to be safe; greyhounds, like other dogs, are at risk when at large—all the more reason to seek out spaces to allow them to do what they are bred to do. Selective breeding is a dynamic process and many breeds described in history have been lost to us because of changing needs, neglect or natural attrition. Providing companionship benefits human existence immeasurably—but let's not forget to leave the dog in dog.

Good socialization, ongoing socialization, is required for a well-mannered dog. Leash laws have the unintended habit of isolating dogs from one another. If you have qualms about dog parks find a time when the dog-traffic is light, or find a bigger dog park. If you have an overprotective dog find friends with dogs with good pack manners. The dog will come to understand that the two, three or four of you are a pack, and that "us" and "them" doesn't mean that other dogs are adversaries. Being relaxed and happy to see other dogs starts with you.

If you think you have a dog that doesn't need much exercise think again. Exercise contributes to positive mental health—their's and our's. Get out there as much as you can.

The anti-dog coalition that makes our cities dog-unfriendly needs to be beaten back; it robs us of the joy of what it means to be part of the animal family. Canada, take a lesson from Europe, where a well-behaved dog is welcome in a restaurant. Some American restaurants have started to allow dogs into outside dining areas; that's a start. Bring-Your-Dog-To-Work Day should be embraced as part of the joy of diversity.

Why not lift the bans that prevent dogs from being in the places where people live, work and thrive? We don't condone child-free public spaces so why accept dog-free ones? Bylaws that are intolerant of dogs make us a less tolerant society in general, and less knowledgeable too. The things we love most about dogs—that they make us laugh, run and play, notice the sun, inspire kindness, rehearse reliability and practice trust—are lost if we don't make them a part of our social environments.

Finally, there is something wrong with a society that recycles dogs. Let's get it together, people!

As Arlette shared with me lately, what we learn from dogs is instinctual and intuitive: trust, respect, teamwork, perseverance, loyalty. What we learn from people about dogs is observational: the high held tail, ascending in position, hierarchical relationships. When it comes to intangibles, like spirit, we often absorb things more unwittingly. It isn't so much that we need to learn these values from dogs, but we do benefit from their example.

Dog-wise people are wise indeed; after all, it is human to reflect upon experience and to extract meaning. No dog offered up his personal philosophy during this inquiry—as plainly as the love of play, treats and a good belly rub speaks for itself.

It is not the experience itself that tells the story, but how we respond to the experience that says something about us. I am very grateful to everyone who shared their time, thoughts and stories about their dogs.

BIBLIOGRAPHY

Andersen, Jodi. The Latchkey Dog, 2000 New York: Harper Collins

Arnold, Jennifer. Through a Dog's Eyes. 2010 New York: Spiegel & Rau

Becker, Marty. The Healing Power of Pets. 2002 New York: Hyperion

Canadian Federation of Human Societies, Humane Societies and SPCAs in Canada: A Comprehensive Look at the Sector, 2016

Canadian Federation of Human Societies, Animal Shelters Statistics 2015, December 14, 2016.

Canadian Kennel Club, accessed 2015 http://www.ckc.ca/en

Coren, Stanley. How Dogs Think. 2004 New York: Simon & Schuster

Coren, Stanley. The Intelligence of Dogs. Toronto: Maxwell MacMillan; 1994.

Grandin, Temple and Johnson, Catherine. Animals in translation. 2005 New York: Harcourt

Grandin, Temple and Johnson, Catherine. Animals Make Us Human. 2010 New York: Mariner

Horowitz, Alexandra. Inside of a Dog, What Dogs See, Smell, and Know. 2009 New York: Scribner

Kotler, Steven. A Small Furry Prayer: Dog Rescue and the Meaning of Life. 2010 New York: Bloomsbury

Police Dog Service Training Centre, Royal Canadian Mounted Police accessed 2014 http://www.rcmp-grc.gc.ca/depot/pdstc-cdcp/index-eng.htm

Ranching with Sheep blog accessed 2015 http://ranching-with-sheep.blogspot.ca/

Schmutz, Joe. Hunting Dog Ingredients. The Pointing Dog Journal 2007; 15 2:xx-xx

Seib, Arlette, 2014 Guardian Dogs and Management Practices to Help Coexist with Predators, accessed 2014

http://www.ranching-with-sheep.com/support-files/guardian-dogs-and-flock-management.pdf
Suzuki, David CBC Nature of Things, A Dog's Life, Sept 2, 2014
http://www.cbc.ca/player/Shows/Shows/The+Nature+of+Things/2013-14/ID/2419799184/
Thomas, Elizabeth Marshall. The Social Lives of Dogs. 2000 New York: Simon & Schuster
Thomas, Elizabeth Marshall. The Hidden Life of Dogs. 1993 New York: Houghton Mifflin
Wall, C. Denise and DeMille, Mellissa. Heritability of Herding-Related Traits, 1996
http://www.stilhope.com/writings/heritability.html

JUDITH WRIGHT

ABOUT THE AUTHOR

Judith Wright is a Saskatchewan writer who has worked as a Public Health epidemiologist for fifteen years. She is the author of the novel, *The Magpie Summer*. Her stories have appeared in a variety of magazines, including *Grain*, *Fiddlehead*, *Prairies North*, *The Gardener*, *Western Producer* and *Harrowsmith*. She is interested in ordinary wisdom—how insight gained from everyday experience informs the way the wider world is viewed. She is working on a second non-fiction book about what our gardens reveal about us. She and Tove divide their time between Saskatoon and Val Marie.

Author photo by James R. Page

For more, see: www.authorjudithwright.ca

This author's proof may contain small errors
that will be corrected in final publication